Praise for *BIG Ideas to BIG Results*, First Edition

"This book is a must read for leaders building focused and strategically driven businesses. Mike and Bob, the knowledge practice leaders in transformation leadership, here provide important insights for managers who aspire to impact the direction of their organizations."

—**John W. Spiegel**, Chairman, S1 Corporation, and Former Vice Chairman and Chief Financial Officer, SunTrust Banks, Inc.

"*BIG Ideas to BIG Results* is Must Reading. Mike and Robert have honed the Accelerated Corporate Transformation Process based on innovative thinking and extensive real world corporate transformation experience."

—**Sam Araki**, CEO, ST-Infonox, and Former President, Lockheed-Martin Missiles and Space

"Kanazawa and Miles provide you with a roadmap for success. They show you how to keep it simple, communicate the vision, and execute all levels of the organization."

—**Peter L. Lynch**, Chairman, CEO, and President, Winn-Dixie Stores, Inc.

"I really like the frank, plain talking, honest approach. Many of the points Mike and Bob make match my experiences so I found myself smiling a lot as I read through the chapters. I would recommend this book to the CEOs I work with."

—**Kevin Compton**, Partner, Kleiner Perkins Caufield & Byers

"Short, simple, and to the point. Kanazawa and Miles distill decades of corporate transformation experience down to a few, vital messages. Required reading for CEOs."

—**Peter Darbee**, Chairman, CEO, and President, PG&E Corporation

"Mike and Bob have outlined an extensive and highly valuable set of actions and processes that can be implemented by corporate management to drive significant improvement in organizations. Their approach can be of great benefit not only to CEOs and their executive staffs, but also to vice presidents, general managers, and department heads."

—**Richard Beyer**, President and CEO, Intersil Corporation

"This book is a must read for CEOs who are looking for time-tested principles and a proven process by which senior teams can realign their organization and its people with their strategic intent. In a fast moving world, nothing is more important."

—**Michael Beer**, Cahners-Raab Professor of Business, Harvard Business School and author, *Breaking the Code of Change*

"*BIG Ideas to BIG Results* is a must read for CEOs, as well as managers empowered with bringing about meaningful change. Most executives are comfortable with functional change within their own areas of competence and responsibilities, but one of the most challenging realities of the 21st century is that competitive advantage and speed of change require complex cross-functional solutions. I am recommending reading this book to all of my C-level clients."

—**Jerry Black**, President and CEO, Kurt Salmon Associates

"In the past years as a new General Manager and then as a new CEO, I have had the pleasure of working with Bob and Mike on corporate transformation challenges. They have done an outstanding job of distilling complex corporate turnaround principles into a practical book full of blueprints for CEOs, their executive staffs, and their boards to apply in corporate transformations."

—**Dr. Bami Bastani**, President and CEO, Anadigics, Inc.

"ACT: an amalgamation of time-tested wisdom, frameworks, processes, and illustrative cases that provides a must read for both successful companies and those that are in transition. Everything is right here in this Little Red Book, for the CEO down to the managers of companies that need to execute."

—**Mas Sakamoto**, Vice President, Corporate Planning and Marketing, NEC Corporation of America

"*BIG Ideas to BIG Results* is a superb handbook for leaders wanting to transform their organizations. With Bob Miles' expert guidance, our company launched a transformation four years ago, and our Drive for Value business model is now embedded in the way we operate."

—**Shirley Gaufin**, Chief Human Resources Officer, Black & Veatch

"For the past ten years, leader-led techniques have helped us transform Delta TechOps from a cost center to the largest maintenance repair and overhaul center in North America. Mike and Bob make it simple and easy to execute."

—**Anthony Charaf**, Senior Vice President, TechOps, Delta Air Lines, Inc.

"ACT was employed at the Tour a decade and a half ago to help the new commissioner 'take charge' and most recently to relaunch the Nationwide Tour. It is simple, it gets the job done rapidly, and it can be adapted to any corporate transformation challenge."

—Worth W. Calfee, President, Nationwide Tour of the PGA Tour

"An important reading for any executive who wants to revitalize his/her company, and do it efficiently!"

—Jay W. Lorsch, Louis E. Kirstein Professor of Human Relations, Harvard Business School

"*BIG Ideas to BIG Results* captures a very simple but powerful methodology for transforming ideas into action. Their recipe for leadership really moves the corporate mountain."

—John Baker, CEO and President, Florida Rock Industries, Inc.

"*BIG Ideas to BIG Results* shows how to take strategies and connect them with tactics, align an entire organization around a common set of goals, and get everyone bought in. It is the one ingredient most companies miss, and this is the one that helps you win."

—Tony Weiss, Vice President/General Manager, Software, Peripherals, Imaging, Displays, and Dell Direct Retail, Dell, Inc.

"*BIG Ideas to BIG Results* is chock full of practical tools to get your strategy and operations in synch and moving faster down the track—a 'do more on less' guidebook for every executive."

—Marty Beard, President, Sybase 365

"Want to improve your valuation? Get your ACT in gear. This book is highly recommended reading for executives who understand that higher market values are commanded by those companies that consistently generate big ideas and convert those ideas into big results."

—Michael Gardner, Executive Vice President, Wedbush Morgan Securities

"Having experienced guidance from Mike on his process for strategic transformation in our business unit, I must confess that I am now reconciled with strategic business consultants! This book is a must-read for any executive willing to engage into a reshaping of its organization for a more ambitious future."

—Olivier Le Peuch, President, Schlumberger Information Solutions

"Our executive clients consistently ask for tools, rather than theory, that they can immediately implement in order to execute strategy. *BIG Ideas to BIG Results* offers a uniquely clear and practical format for confronting and transforming reality with proven results."

—**Whitney Hischier**, Assistant Dean, Center of Executive Development, Haas School of Business, University of California at Berkeley

"*BIG Ideas to BIG Results* describes a powerful yet simple way for leaders to reposition a company in a highly efficient manner, critical in today's fast-paced, everchanging, 'flat' world. It produces clear measurable results, energizes and aligns everyone in the organization, and is the only methodology I have experienced where everything you do is an integral part of your job—period!"

—**Javed Patel**, CEO, Sierra Monolithics

"It's one part strategic focus, one part business operations, one part leadership, and one part employee engagement. Mike and Bob show you the streamlined, simple, and potent recipe for combining these elements to turn your big strategic ideas into real business results."

—**Pascal Lenoir**, CEO, NagraStar

"*BIG Ideas to BIG Results* is a must read for every CEO, offering a practical approach to alignment and engagement that will result in unbelievable transformation. This book is easy reading and is full of great case studies that will inspire every person in a business leadership role."

—**Carlo Saggese**, Vice President of Application Development, Vistage International—The world's leading chief executive organization

"Kanazawa and Miles provide an easy to relate account of some often paradoxical issues with large corporations. The authors provide sound advice in a book which can be easily read on a long flight."

—**Peters Suh**, President, Vodafone Asia Pacific Ltd and Vodafone Ventures Ltd

"Mike Kanazawa and Bob Miles lay out a powerful, proven process for leaders at all levels. With a focus on alignment and engaging the entire organization, this book is an excellent resource for leaders who want to drive results."

—**Ann Marie Beasley**, Vice President, Office of Strategy Management, Symantec Corporation

"This is a must-have handbook for any leader guiding an organization through strategic change. It provides practical insights that ensure the entire organization understands its role in fulfilling the strategic aims of the business. Too many transformational frameworks rely on a top-down approach; this book helps you ensure all the oars are in the water and rowing together."

—**Matt DiMaria**, Chief Marketing Officer, Sonic Solutions

"I love the topic the book is addressing. Its approach simplifies the recipe for success for any business, large or small, private or public, from the aspect of making ideas produce results. Too often, we as corporate executives go out of our way to complicate the planning and implementation process. It is obvious that the authors have witnessed this tragedy over and over, as their writing is filled with practical examples of 'how-to' bridge ineffective scenarios to become high-performing environments."

—**Esther de Wolde**, CEO, Phantom Screens

"Whether your organization numbers 10 or 10,000, you owe it to yourself and your team to read this book! The proven process will enable you to refocus your organization, implement lasting change, and produce sustained superior results."

—**Rob Koteskey**, airline captain, naval officer, and team performance consultant

"Big ideas are the easy part. Getting big results requires the joint efforts of all, and not just going through the motions or going along with the flow. *BIG Ideas to BIG Results* provides the recipe for combining your big ideas with an inspired and engaged team. Simply put, it just works."

—**Larry Mondry**, CEO, CSK Auto

"*BIG Ideas to BIG Results* strikes a balance that is very difficult to achieve in that it's not so rigid as to seem artificial, yet not so flexible as to lack conviction. This book provides real, sound advice."

—**Bill Hopkins**, Managing Principal, Odyssey Investment Partners

"*BIG Ideas to BIG Results* provides leaders with a solution that instills confidence, purpose, and alignment throughout an entire organization and spikes it with a bias for speed and ACTion. The ACT 'leader-led' process is a dramatic departure from traditional consulting methods in that it unleashes value creators at every level of an organization."

—**George A. Coll**, SVP, New Services, Sears Holdings Corporation

BIG Ideas to BIG Results

Leading Corporate Transformation
in a Disruptive World

BIG Ideas to BIG Results

Leading Corporate Transformation in a Disruptive World

Second Edition

Robert H. Miles | Michael T. Kanazawa

Publisher: Paul Boger
Editor-in-Chief: Amy Neidlinger
Cover Designer: Alan Clements
Managing Editor: Kristy Hart
Senior Project Editor: Andy Beaster
Copy Editor: Chrissy White
Proofreader: Chuck Hutchinson
Indexer: Tim Wright
Compositor: Nonie Ratcliff
Manufacturing Buyer: Dan Uhrig

For information about buying this title in bulk quantities, or for special sales opportunities (which may include electronic versions; custom cover designs; and content particular to your business, training goals, marketing focus, or branding interests), please contact our corporate sales department at corpsales@pearsoned.com or (800) 382-3419.

For government sales inquiries, please contact governmentsales@pearsoned.com.

For questions about sales outside the U.S., please contact international@pearsoned.com.

Company and product names mentioned herein are the trademarks or registered trademarks of their respective owners.

Printed in the United States of America

First Printing: December 2015

ISBN-10: 0-13-419384-9
ISBN-13: 978-0-13-419384-7

Pearson Education LTD.
Pearson Education Australia PTY, Limited.
Pearson Education Singapore, Pte. Ltd.
Pearson Education Asia, Ltd.
Pearson Education Canada, Ltd.
Pearson Educación de Mexico, S.A. de C.V.
Pearson Education—Japan
Pearson Education Malaysia, Pte. Ltd.

Library of Congress Control Number: 2015953288

To the future:
Miles Curtius Lewis
and
Katharina Anna-Sophia Miles
With love,
—Bob

To my wife and children and the life we share,
to John Dare and David Takeuchi and the businesses
we built and to co-workers and clients
for the experiences we create. ...
—Mike

Contents

Preface

Corporate transformation is tough work, but extraordinarily rewarding for all involved when led successfully. Somebody's got to do it, and do it well. What if that someone happens to be you? Where will you start? How will you frame your transformation game plan and lay out its roadmap? What will you do first, and who will you engage when in the enterprise? How will you keep it alive after the early excitement? And how will you make it part of your management process so that it can become a reliable core competency for rising to the increasing rate of disruptive transformation challenges facing your company?

Leading Rapid Corporate Transformations in a Disruptive World

Getting from *BIG Ideas to BIG Results* was the promise of our first book, and it remains so in this second edition. In the first edition we focused on sharing insights gleaned from over two decades of intensive support of dozens of successful CEO-led corporate transformations. In this edition, we want to respond to the many requests from readers for guidance on how to lead a rapid transformation, step by step. The book has been reorganized—indeed, transformed—from a topical exploration of rapid corporate transformations into a roadmap of chapters that actually reveal the required phases of work.

The second reason for writing the new edition has to do with dramatic changes that have taken place in the decade since we first put our *BIG Ideas to BIG Results* pens on paper. The frequency and intensity of disruptive innovations are increasing, emphasizing the importance to the fundamental capability of leaders to drive corporate transformations and leading to new accelerators and innovations to how transformations are realized. Today, transformations require purpose, a clear focus on customer experience, design, agility, and an ability to engage digitally connected stakeholders inside and outside of the formal organization. We have continued to evolve our approach by incorporating accelerators that have allowed companies to stay a step ahead of the megatrends that are reshaping the business environment and the constant onrush of disruptive new competitors.

In this new book, we have attempted to take the complexity out of leading corporate transformations, thereby enabling you to speed it up to keep everyone's attention and realize early breakthrough results. This simplified format and streamlined roadmap are not only essential to guide Chief Executive Officers, but they are also critical for the success of the senior leaders who report to the CEO as well as of the leaders of the business and functional units that must implement the transformation initiatives. Understanding this same streamlined approach is also important for the managers and employees throughout the enterprise in order to translate the corporate transformation game plan for execution in relevant ways in their areas of responsibility. Finally, staff professionals, who are called upon to support the implementation of a corporate transformation, will find this simplified and compressed approach uniquely effective in engaging the corporate community and accelerating its performance and learning cycle.

Each chapter in the streamlined transformation roadmap outlines the essential steps and specific interventions and embeds them in actual case studies so they may be observed in action. If an executive leader rapidly paces an organization through these steps, he or she will be able to significantly raise the probability of achieving the early breakthrough results that are targeted in their transformation game plan.

We have developed and refined over the decades a methodology for enabling CEOs and executive leaders to rise to a wide variety of corporate transformation challenges—one that is perfectly horizontal, meaning that it works in every industry and setting in which we have applied it. We often say that it represents simplicity on the other side of transformation complexity. The latest version of the methodology is called *Accelerated Corporate Transformation*, or *ACT*.

For quite some time now, successfully leading an organization through a corporate transformation has consistently been one of the most significant challenges for executives to navigate in their careers. But today's competitive disruptions are coming faster and with greater severity. This means that leaders and their organizations must now become effective at continuously transforming departments and entire businesses, not just once every five to ten years. Creating a leadership team and organization that can, first, achieve and then maintain this level of strategic agility over time has become an essential corporate competency.

Even though our practice has been almost exclusively devoted to CEO-led corporate transformations, the principles and the transformation game plans we have derived from the great variety of corporate transformation challenges, as you will see from the case examples we report, also work for transformation leaders of business units and functional departments. Indeed, many of the embedded ACT principles and techniques are applicable in the final analysis to the manner in which supervisors and first-line employees can more effectively plan and execute their jobs. They actually get trained in these techniques through participation in an ACT-based corporate transformation as part of what we refer to as a *Trojan Horse* for management development.

With all of the fundamental changes around us and desire to uncover the stepwise process, we saw a need to more deeply elucidate and illustrate in this book what is still forever true about transforming organizations and also share the newer disruptive innovations to the way corporate transformation approaches are being shaped by these same megatrends. Our continued work, side-by-side with executives in leading corporate transformations, has given us the ability to validate the fundamentals of transformation that have been true as long as people have been organizing and creating businesses and better understand some of the new wrinkles to transformation in this age of innovation and disruption.

We enjoyed hearing from you about the first book, without which we would not have written the "transformed" new edition. Given the more operational tack in the new edition, we look forward to hearing about how you adapted and deployed the ACT-based approach to your transformation challenges and turned disruption into opportunity. We will also be on the lookout for any additional lessons you have to share about increasing the simplicity on the other side of transformation complexity.

1

Accelerated Corporate Transformation: The Foundations

In this world of disruption and innovation, the need to drive sustained growth and profits and generate results through consistent execution of strategy are the top challenges noted by CEOs. To rise to these challenges, leaders at all levels need to execute large-scale transformations, while at the same time delivering short-term results every day. As you will soon see, corporate transformations usually boil down to "a few well-articulated initiatives targeted for breakthrough results in a short period of time...in a sea of necessary incremental improvements."[1]

Achieving this balance is one of the most difficult challenges you will face as a leader in your career and one of the most rewarding when you get it right. And the challenge has become more acute than before imagined. Until recently, it was generally recognized most executive leaders got to rise to a corporate transformation challenge only once in a career. With little practice beforehand, the odds of success in these previously uncharted waters was slim. Those who could pull off such a feat became the CEO icons of their age.

But today's universal compression of cycle times across almost all industries is creating waves of transformation challenges in rapid succession that have had two major consequences for the guidance available to executive leaders to ensure success. Even industries previously insulated from big swings in fortune have had to yield to the speedup and compression of many aspects of their business as a derivative of the march of new technology. First, the speed with which transformation must achieve breakthrough success has greatly accelerated. Put simply, transformations must be both bold and rapid to be successful. Second, the compression of successive waves of potentially disruptive competitive forces has created an environment in which companies must build the competence for leading transformations deeply into the marrow of their management process. Where once it was sufficient to transform something to a target future state, now that once-acquired transformational competence must be enabled to permeate the entire enterprise so as to make it continuously agile in anticipating and adapting to new challenges.

Transformation has been used to describe everything from high-risk overhauls of a business to tactical changes in IT systems. So to be clear, by *transformation*, we mean a wide range of actions and opportunities required to drive continuous prosperity in a business. These range from a new leader "taking charge," to launching a new phase in the organization, to entering new markets, to integrating major acquisitions, to breaking down silos to operate as "one company," to boldly launching a major strategic initiative.

This is tough work, and most efforts fall short.

Imagine you are the leader of an organization and you are about to launch a corporate transformation or shift in strategic direction. Your executive team has just completed a set of anonymous interviews with an objective third party. You're looking over the results as you prepare with your leadership to launch a transformation effort intended to ensure the company's next growth phase. You wonder how to respond to anonymous quotes like the following:

- "We never follow through on anything all the way to see if it will produce results. We launch things, and then when they don't immediately turn results, we just start launching more things."
- "We are the best at being second best."

- "There should not be 20 initiatives; we should focus on a very few things."

- "We have organizational attention deficit disorder, starting at the top."

These are actual quotes from senior executives at some of our multibillion dollar clients who were calling for a shift to a new level of play. Not too encouraging when you are trying to drive a major strategic shift in direction to achieve breakthrough results. These quotes, while alarming, are being expressed in all corners of organizations today. Why do so many high-achieving leaders feel this sense of dread when confronted with the challenge to take things to the next level? Why all the frustration and skepticism?

The need for these major course corrections and interventions to break the status quo—for corporate transformations—is coming in one wave after another because of the challenges of rapid earnings growth expectations, globalization, commoditization of markets, and executive turnover rates, as well as from challenges from activist investors.

How are we doing with these challenges? Not great. Based on data from a poll of 11,000 workers, fewer than half of employees understand their company's strategic goals, less than 25% feel their organization sets goals that people are enthusiastic about, only 38% believe their planning results in clear assignments for individuals, and 43% feel there isn't any follow-through on the plans anyway. Whoa! Not a fertile field upon which to nurture a major transformation.

The range of methods for attempting to lead transformations is as varied as transformation challenges themselves. Some leaders resort to dramatic communication "campaigns," believing that if people can just "get it," they will "get on with it." Others attempt to grease the skids of a transformation launch with a barrage of tactical change management and training interventions. Others quickly turn their transformation over to program management offices and then move on to other issues. And still other leaders scorecard everything in sight because of their gut belief in measurement and delegation.

Clearly, each of these and many other management orthodoxies contain elements that can contribute to corporate transformation success. But none of these more operational and tactical approaches were designed from the outset to handle all of the key moving parts in an enterprise-wide, top-to-bottom, corporate transformation. However, within the orchestration of a proven corporate transformation game plan, many of these tactical methodologies can play an important supporting role—as long as they take their lead from the corporate transformation plan and roadmap that we are about to introduce.

Tactical Is Not Transformative

Let's pause briefly to examine how one of these potentially useful tactical approaches failed to deliver the whole of a corporate transformation.

A typical mid-cap corporation needed to transform to meet new competitive pressures. The senior executive pulled a small team together to build a plan based on industry best practices focused on process and systems enhancements that were targeted at operational savings in Finance, IT, HR, Supply Chain, and other functional areas. A small group of internal analysts provided data to the team to build a financial model that promised to save hundreds of millions of dollars in operating expenses, based on applying ratios of the best practices to the company's financials. These huge expected savings, then taken as a given, would provide much room for investing in reorganization and systems implementations to achieve the savings. With a huge expected return on investment firmly established, the executives signed up to launch the transformation effort.

Right off the bat, rows of cubicles were set up to make room for a newly funded transformation team of process and systems experts to do their work. Bright and energetic people showed up with great credentials and fantastic analytical skills. They polled managers to build process maps of the current state of the business. Then they applied their "knowledge base" to create a future state of the business, which, of course, included the many organization and systems upgrades they had proposed.

A year into the process, it was time for the organization changes and systems to be rolled out to the "troops." Blank-faced line managers were now told to "buy in" and start producing the hundreds of millions of dollars in expected savings by implementing the new organization structure, systems, and processes. The money was already spent, so there was no turning back. Unfortunately, the managers weren't fully engaged in the process and had never agreed with many of the suggested changes. In fact, some of the most high-leverage systems and process changes had not even been addressed because they weren't a part of the rollout, and the organization changes actually created new problems bigger than the ones they intended to solve. Solutions based on external best practices turned out to be impractical. They didn't take into consideration how work was actually done in that particular company or their unique approach to customer experience. The process stalled while the rollout team struggled with numerous meetings to listen to the troops' concerns. By that time, of course, it was too late to make expensive adjustments on a timely basis, and the transformation careened out of control.

Seeing the impasse, the senior executive decided that an internal person should take point because the troops were beginning to reject the entire transformation program. So, two years into the process, a high-potential, upper middle manager was named transformation "czar." The poor, unsuspecting high potential manager, of course, had little operational clout but fought valiantly in a last-ditch effort to regain momentum for the transformation effort. But, in the end, the effort died a slow death. Some savings showed up as aggressive layoffs. Redeployments caused people to have to do "more with less."

And a few of the systems changes actually worked. However, the result was far from transformational. It was chalked up by the troops as another "flavor of the month"—just one more layer of projects and programs adding to the overload and gridlock they already faced. Or as one manager called it, *"Just another sugar high."* Another quick peaking activity followed by a crash.

And what typically happens next? Management sees the lack of results and looks for the next new thing to launch, while employees become even more skeptical and unwilling to salute each successive clarion for change. The high-potential czar is shown the door.

Most of us have seen this type of effort play out similarly to the curve shown in Figure 1.1.

Figure 1.1 Typical Cycle of Failure

Nobody is immune to the kinds of rapidly changing market conditions that create the need for these bold calls to action, just as nobody can avoid the macro business cycles that make fortunes rise and fall. And special transformation teams certainly have the ability to help in a more productive way if placed in the correct supporting roles where their true expertise is leveraged. The real question from this description of a sad but all-too-common story: How can we break this cycle? How can we lay out a corporate transformation game plan up front that allows everyone to understand, relate, and commit to performing his or her role in an aligned and energetic manner? How can we orchestrate a leader-led transformation? And how can we sustain the early high level of energy and focus throughout the Execution Phase?

Get Your ACT Together

More than 25 years ago, groups of CEOs, division presidents, and their executive teams gathered for two weeks to participate in an innovative program at the Harvard Business School. There, they would work collaboratively on their top business challenge with non-competing peers and key faculty. Spending time in the hallowed halls of ivy was not at all a time-out from real business for intellectual theorizing. While sequestered on the Harvard campus, they would help each other build action plans that they would implement back home. They would then return nine months later to describe to their peer group how the solutions worked and how they could be improved.

After several years of the program, a clear pattern emerged. The biggest and most common problem facing executives was in leading different types of corporate transformations. They had trouble getting their organizations to execute on their stated strategies quickly. The rudiments of the process that resulted, later refined over decades and now known as *ACT (Accelerated Corporate Transformation)*, was conceived through the ideas and trials by these groups of leaders. Its value proposition reads as follows:

ACT is a proven, enterprise-level process architecture. It enables an executive leader to rapidly orchestrate the launch of the next major phase in his or her organization in a simple, high-engagement manner to achieve breakthrough results.[2]

The Origins of ACT

The ACT (Accelerated Corporate Transformation) process was originally distilled by Dr. Robert H. Miles through the innovative "Managing Organizational Effectiveness" program, which he chaired at the Harvard Business School. This process architecture was developed through work with top executives and their teams wrestling with the realities of how to rise to the major challenge confronting their organization. The process was refined as he served over the next two decades as the principal process architect of over 30 successful CEO-led corporate transformations. It continues to be refined by Michael Kanazawa and Dr. Miles through their collaborative work with executive leaders facing a variety of corporate transformation challenges.

The ACT process architecture has been designed to quickly focus, align and engage the full organization, and then rigorously follow through for execution. It was also designed to be run by business leaders with only light consulting and implementation support the first time through. By design it allows managers at all levels to effectively lead organizational transformation and strategy execution on their own.

Over the years, countless leaders and teams have leveraged the same process and refined and streamlined it with their contributions.

By keeping the responsibility for leading the transformation squarely in the hands of business leaders themselves, the result is not only quantum improvement in the targeted initiatives in a shorter-than-expected period of time, but also a fundamental improvement in the leadership acumen from top to bottom in the organization. Through experience across many transformations, it is clear that each of the ACT process steps counts and, hence, should not be sidestepped. However, the manner in which you and your team lead the organization through the steps really makes the difference. For this reason, in the core chapters of this book, the keys to success are largely conveyed through the stories told by the leaders who have used the ACT process architecture to successfully generate large-scale breakthroughs while driving short-term execution and results.

Following are three examples of the dramatic shifts in performance that are possible, even at a very large scale, within a matter of months (not years). The companies profiled implemented and adopted the ACT process into their operating and management models to quickly generate their breakthrough results. In comparison to the typical cycle of failure, these successful efforts looked like the curve in Figure 1.2 where focus and energy were built early and then sustained, leading to compounding growth in results.

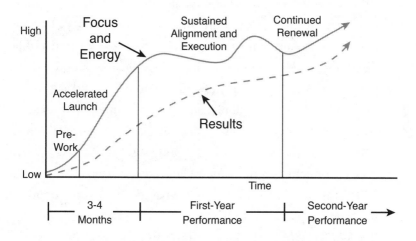

Figure 1.2 Business Cycle of Success

- Twelve months after it failed to merge with a major competitor, the new, internally promoted CEO of a major global retailer faced a huge challenge: to rapidly revitalize the company's sagging retail operations. The company's leaders resolved to once again make the company the industry's most compelling place to *invest, shop,* and *work.* Indeed, these became the major transformation initiatives upon which the company's revitalization was launched. They succeeded. In a year, the company's share price jumped by 156%, customer complaints fell by 50%, and employee retention rates rose by 72%. The company also moved up from the bottom 10% of the Standard & Poor's 500 to number two in terms of percentage increase in shareholder value. *"The biggest surprise,"* the CEO reflected, *"was how*

quickly people in our company said, 'Count me in. Let's go.'
I knew it would happen; I just didn't think we'd get there this
fast."

- One of the largest electric utilities in the U.S. needed to transform its major production function, which consisted of fossil fuel and hydroelectric power plants spread over several geographically dispersed operating companies, each with its own union, into a single, new generation company (or GenCo). Changing from a confederation of line units within a regulated public utility into a self-contained, competitive business required the GenCo to learn a whole new way of thinking and acting, all under the white-hot light of a nationally prominent parent company that was acclaimed as *Fortune* magazine's "Most Admired" company in the utility industry and was the nation's largest power company at the time. The makeover involved almost 100 plants and over 50,000 union-based employees reporting to several separate subsidiaries, and the feat was accomplished in the middle of a CEO transition. After the repositioning, the company's operating costs plunged by more than $100 million in a year and over $300 million in three years, while accidents were cut by 30% and union grievances fell by 72%. Employee morale soared as well.

- Once a vibrant Silicon Valley high-tech company, a global high-tech software leader had stopped growing. Sales had stagnated at a little less than a half billion per year, largely because its past strategy of acquiring companies for growth had run its full course. In fact, all of the best targets in the market had been acquired, and future growth would require a different strategy based on internal innovations. With strong leadership and the simple ACT-based transformation process, this software leader managed to fold its disconnected subsidiaries into one smoothly integrated business focused on customer needs. The new customer focus and highly engaged team revived innovation, inspired new products, and triggered steady sales growth worldwide. In the first year alone, the company improved morale, slashing employee turnover by 41%, while its stock price rose by 53%, its revenue jumped by 24%, and its profitability soared by 290%.

The key differences in these successful efforts compared to the typical failed effort can be seen by comparing the success versus failure cycles in Figure 1.3. The keys are generating a tight focus and an accelerated, high employee engagement launch up front and then maintaining alignment and follow-through for the remainder of the performance year. The transformation phases have to be carefully orchestrated by senior leadership. With that kind of corporate transformation game plan in place, it comes down to consistency in driving the process on an annual basis to continually stretch performance.

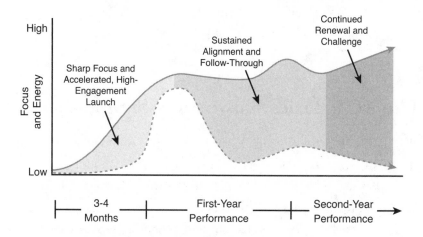

Figure 1.3 Key Differences Between Success and Failure

Make Transformation a Simple Routine

Overall, driving transformations and dramatic shifts in performance is hard work. Old habits die hard. In transformation work there are many moving parts and tough decisions to make. But if you are intent on breaking your organization free of mediocrity or sending it in a bold, new direction, you can profit from the insights of leaders who have succeeded in doing just that in the chapters that follow. If you put the right process in place, it will handle 90% of all of the lessons, keys to success, and subtle warning flags to which you need to pay attention. Then you can spend your time thinking strategically, working closely with your leadership team, and communicating clearly with all your employees—the key areas where you can provide the most value.

The surprisingly simple ACT-based process architecture can be put in place to bring all of the critical principles into play. It contains the foundational elements for simply and reliably leading a rapid and successful corporate transformation. Most of the remaining chapters lay out in sequence the foundational accelerators that you need to deploy, starting with the Launch Phase and continuing all the way through the Execution and Replanning Phases.[3]

So let's take a closer look at ACT.

The ACT Basics: Powerfully Simple

The ACT process itself does not look too exciting or different on the surface. Many people sharing advice and methodologies have maps that will look almost identical to the untrained eye. However, there are big differences when you go to use them; just as two pieces of music can look very similar on paper, one creates beauty when played, and the other creates dissonant noise. On the surface, both scores will have notes, bars (the lines where the notes sit), and different markings that are the basics of music. But if the notes aren't in the correct sequence and timing and played in the correct key and note combinations, it will just produce noise. One of the pieces of music in Figure 1.4 is the first part of Mozart's *Eine Kleine Nachtmusik* (A Little Night Music), a beautiful song. The other is noise, given a few subtle changes and errors. Can you tell which is which? Clearly, some musicians and experts will immediately know, but it is tough to tell on the surface. If we played them both through for you, you'd immediately know for sure. The second one sounds really awful.

Figure 1.4 Harmony or Cacophony?

Consider the ACT process architecture a symphony that has continuously been played through, improved, and boiled down to the essentials over years of productive work and active use. Each time a new leader uses it, he or she turns another crank on streamlining the process that's been going through refinement for over 30 years. So, the fact that it is simple and not some Rube Goldberg type of process with a million extra moving parts with fancy names is intentional and took hard work. Each part has been simplified and optimally sequenced, and it plays off the other parts in an intentional way in which you as a transformation leader can depend. The methodology is perfectly horizontal. It has never met an industry vertical for which it did not succeed.

In its simplest expression the *Accelerated Corporate Transformation*, or *ACT*, process architecture takes the form illustrated in Figure 1.5. The highlighted elements are what we refer to as the *Foundational* elements that are necessary for effectively leading a rapid transformation.

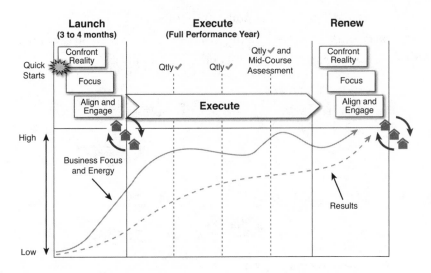

Figure 1.5 ACT Process Architecture

Source: Copyright © by Robert H. Miles, Corporate Transformation Resources, 2001. Permission granted.

The basic ACT-based plan starts with the Launch Phase, compressed into a few months that goes from clarifying the purpose, strategic vision, business success model, company values, and corporate transformation initiatives, as well as some obvious "Quick Starts" to get the process moving while planning proceeds. The Launch Phase consists of a series of steps, starting with confronting reality, focus, and alignment, which ends with a transition to the Cascade Phase, which rapidly engages the full organization, and which enables and engages managers and employees at all levels to translate the corporate transformation constructs into individual commitments to action that are relevant for their level and job scope. ACT accomplishes this rollout with its unique *Rapid, High-engagement, All-employee Cascade*™ methodology and tools.

The cascade is followed by a longer Execution Phase that puts in place quarterly leadership performance checkpoints to hold accountabilities, share best practices across the businesses and departments, and make mid-course adjustments in an agile way when needed. Each quarterly checkpoint is quickly followed by a mini-cascade that enables all managers and employees to make timely refinements in their commitments to further accelerate the corporate transformation.

Finally, there is a Renew Phase at the end of the first performance year under ACT, which is designed to refresh the corporate transformation initiatives in light of actual achievements and associated organizational learning. This phase engages *everyone* in a relaunch of the ACT-based corporate transformation process, although in a more streamlined manner than was possible the first time through.

The top of Figure 1.5 shows a graphic of the full process architecture; the bottom of the figure shows how the organizational energy and focus are built and sustained over time. Notice that the process steps are designed and sequenced specifically to maintain the business focus and energy at the correct level to drive results over the course of the first full performance cycle, usually one year. When implemented without skipping its few simple steps, the ACT process creates energy and momentum, as well as an acceleration of business performance and culture change as it is integrated into the business operations.

Creating Safe Passage—A Clear Transformation Process

Before leaving this introduction to ACT, we want to highlight the importance of its first step, *"Creating Safe Passage."*

The first key to effectively launching a tight corporate transformation game plan is to make sure that everyone understands the path that will be followed and how and where they fit in. It is fun to say that "we need a burning platform" to get people moving. It sounds decisive. You might get people scrambling out of fear, but that is not the kind of energy you need to create to be successful.

Before "lighting the fire," you need to make sure that there is a clear and *safe passage* from the state of things today to the new state or strategic direction. Safe passage does not mean that 100% of the people will keep their jobs or that all budgets will remain intact. Everyone knows and understands the realities of making tough trade-offs to refocus a business. So, above all, be honest if there are these types of tough decisions that will need to be made. All that is expected by your team is that you lay out a very clear process architecture that shows a few critical steps: who will make decisions, when and how people will have input into the decisions, when you will announce final answers, and what will happen as these decisions are made.

There is one qualifier to the term "safe passage" from the perspective of motivating a whole organization to drive the effort. It is not enough to simply lay out your process in advance. Your process needs to be specifically designed for speed and high engagement to be received well and to work. In addition, it is better to set a purposeful "burning ambition" as the motivator to change. Rather than running away from the past based on fear, the idea is to build such a compelling shared purpose and reason for being as a business that employees are magnetized and drawn down the transformation path to pursue the new.

Many processes don't have both the speed and high-engagement elements covered. The typical belief is that to get speed, you can't spend time on communications and dialogue. While under the gun by a board or boss to quickly focus an organization on a new strategic path, it can seem too messy and time consuming to get too many people involved. However to generate a burning ambition in the team necessary to engage fully and continue driving the transformation, it is required. Strategy is not done by consensus, that's true, but it can be done quickly with high engagement. As is typically the case with shortcuts like speeding past engaging the right people up front, things actually end up taking longer because of repeated revisits of past decisions, continued questioning, lack of alignment, and rework. With the right process for engagement up front and leverage of proper technology such as crowd-sourcing and enterprise social media platforms, execution actually goes faster and farther in the end.

A story of a new leader who had been placed in such a position comes to mind. Like many new leaders, he was charged with rapidly turning around the performance of his organization. As a first pass, he and one other executive gathered for a few days with an external consultant to the business and hammered out the new strategy for the company. It was bold, well worded, and to the point. He gathered his VP team to share the document and to get some feedback from them before rolling it out to the entire company.

As he finished reading out the new strategy, the room was absolutely silent. This was uncharacteristic for the hard-driving and outspoken team of executives. He said later that it was one of the worst meetings he recalled being in. He tugged at each of the VPs to obtain a few slight changes to some words, but clearly nobody had any energy or excitement. In fact, they seemed completely disinterested. The team left quietly when the meeting was over. This was the impact of trying to change the direction of the company without the engagement of the right players within the leadership team. It certainly was fast to gather just three people to hammer out the document, but the Senior Leadership Team had no ownership, didn't believe that the right things were considered, and assumed no accountability for making it better. They were being asked to "buy in" to something that they should have been included in building up front.

From there, the leader moved quickly to launch the new strategy through various corporate events and communications, but the people's reception was similar at all levels. Following several months of lackluster execution, the executive team decided to double-back to engage the organization in the strategy development process. Not surprisingly, the result was the complete opposite. The engagement effort re-energized the executive team, who began talking with each other about the business, departmental silos began to disappear, and enthusiasm for the future rebounded radically. As one of the executives put it, "People went from feeling like defeatists back into thinking we could win."

This Is Not a New Religion, Just a Better Way of Managing the Business

We do have a word of caution on launching this type of process. We generally find it necessary to provide an overview of ACT at the beginning of engagement with each level of employees. That seems to be sufficient aside from reminding people when they gather where they stand in terms of waypoints on the transformation roadmap. But ACT is intuitive enough that it doesn't require its own center stage to become operational. As one of our CEO clients once reflected,

> So many other times we would launch programs that were extraneous to our regular jobs. And those other programs were focused just on the executive team. We would come back from one of those off-sites, and everyone on the team would be looking at us suspiciously and questioningly, like 'OK, just tell me what you want me to do now.' With an effective transformation process like ACT, it is not a program. It just becomes the way the business is managed. The process just became our normal management practice as a part of daily life from setting strategy to setting individual personal business commitments and following through on performance.

In the ACT process architecture (refer back to Figure 1.5), you see the essential design elements in the streamlined process architecture. As another seasoned CEO of technology start-ups as well as large companies pointed out following his ACT-based intervention explained,

> Our transformation process was all about taking charge of our future. The process was an opportunity to look at the business

as a whole and ask really tough questions. Instead of defending the status quo, it was more about understanding where the world was going. This type of effort has to be a formal process; otherwise, you won't make the time to address it or the conditions for people to be open minded and self-critical, which are necessary components.

With this brief overview of the ACT process architecture, and its opening gambit of "creating safe passage," the bulk of the subsequent chapters pace you through the transformation roadmap, with each chapter devoted to one of the major phases of this approach to rapid transformation. And each chapter reveals what you need to do to successfully lead your transformation as it unfolds, one step at a time.

We call these ACT steps the *Foundations* of transformation—those few steps that all transformation leaders must master for success. They have been distilled and refined from over 30 years of serving as principal process architects at the right hand of CEOs in over 30 successful corporate transformations.

Tips for Planning an Accelerated Corporate Transformation

- Follow a simple, streamlined process that creates "safe passage" for the full team (easy-to-understand, clear rules of engagement, and is internally led by leaders at all levels).

- Begin with a clear roadmap in place that shows how and when people will be engaged and decisions will be made.

- Leverage a proven corporate transformation process architecture and customize it for your situation.

- Be principally guided by an emphasis on simplicity of content and compression in process.

- Treat your approach to corporate transformation as simply how business will be done, not as a new "religion."

Endnotes

1. Robert H. Miles, "Accelerating Corporate Transformations: A Framework for Success," Corporate Transformation Resources, August 2013, p. 2.

2. Robert H. Miles, "New CEO's 'Taking Charge' Challenge: ACT Solution," Corporate Transformation Resources LLC, White Paper 12-101, May 2012.

3. For a more extensive review of the "Inhibitors" and "Accelerators" of rapid corporate transformation, refer to Robert H. Miles, "Accelerating Corporate Transformations—Don't Lose Your Nerve!" *Harvard Business Review*, January–February 2010; reprinted in the "Reinvention" Edition of HBR OnPoint, Spring 2012.

2

Structuring Your Transformation Launch

At the moment of Launch, the leader of a corporate transformation not only has the greatest ability to shape the design of the whole effort, but also to permanently imprint the culture and management process of the entire enterprise. Just as organizations become imprinted with certain indelible characteristics at the time of their founding, so too do they become demonstrably reshaped in enduring ways by the manner in which their transformations are launched.[1]

All successful transformations must embrace a *structure* or architecture that is inscrutably simple, one that is designed for speed and engagement. They must deploy a *process* that is designed to "create safe passage" for everyone participating in the effort, and that should mean everyone in the organization. These structure and process elements comprise the yin and yang of successful, enterprise-wide transformations.

Imprinting Your Organization

The imprinting of the organization as envisioned in the corporate transformation game plan starts at Launch during the very first meeting of the CEO and the *Senior Leadership Team (SLT)*, and it quickly extends to the third tier of corporate leadership, the *Extended Leadership Team (ELT)*, which is made up of the teams that lead all of the business units and staff departments. By the time the Cascade Phase is completed, everyone in the enterprise is involved, engaged, and committed through immersion in the same corporate transformation game plan, structure, and process that their leaders went through. Moreover, the essence of the ACT-based approach to transformation is absorbed into the day-to-day and year-to-year management process, enabling the enterprise to become more proactive and agile as new transformation challenges and opportunities continue to arise.

To help you see the important and complementary elements of the ACT-based transformation *structure* and *process*, we need to separate them in this and the next chapter. But let's be clear: in the life of a corporate transformation, these essential elements of successful rapid transformations are both inextricable and mutually reinforcing.

As U.S. Supreme Justice Oliver Wendell Holmes is famous for reflecting, "I would not give a fig for the simplicity on this side of complexity, but I would give my life for the simplicity on the other side of complexity." Over years of refinement from an intensive transformation practice, ACT clearly represents the simplicity on the other side of transformation complexity. After you see what the essential core ACT elements are—in terms of both structure and process—you must be careful not to heap on too many other "good ideas," many from well-intentioned managers and staff professionals. Be parsimonious during your transformation Launch. Add to the steps managers and employees have to take only those that are absolutely on the transformation critical path and in keeping with the rapid tempo. Otherwise, you'll dampen the speed on which successful transformations depend and encumber everyone with energy-sapping task overload.

Structuring Rapid Transformations

From the structural perspective, we need to breathe life into four design elements: (1) the overall ACT architecture, including its framework and the all-important transformation roadmap; (2) the

"No-Slack" Launch, the crucible of transformation; (3) the Confronting Reality Encounter; and (4) "Quick Starts." As you will see, the manner in which the Launch is structured soon thereafter sets the template for the rollout to every component, level, and employee in the organization.

We will defer full treatment of the *process* elements, which focus largely on rapidly creating energy, engagement, commitment, and accountability, until the next chapter. And throughout both Launch chapters will be laced the *speed imperative* at the heart of the ACT-based approach. But, as you will discover, we have reserved a special meaning for this term, which permeates everything we do but which is often misunderstood when viewed from a distance.

The No-Slack Launch

How can you effectively collapse the whole Launch process into a short period of time in a meaningful and impactful way, while gaining not only precious time but also essential energy, commitment, and momentum? The "No-Slack Launch," which runs in parallel to the routine management process for a few months, reliably performs this task.[2]

First lay out for the Senior Leadership Team, next for the Extended Leadership Team, and then for all employees, a compressed roadmap with specific waypoints and dates that all will step through on the way to refinement of your new business. Let everyone know what's up and when they will come aboard.

The roadmap needs to be tightly scoped to the essentials of decisions, actions, and outcomes, not an endless list of work activities on a Gantt chart. With proper preparation and good design, you should be able to take your team and the teams reporting directly to them from confronting reality to finalization of the core transformation constructs and initiatives in three to four meetings, interspersed with pre-work and appropriate interim testing and refinements. The roadmap needs to be a compressed one. If team members don't feel they have quite enough time to get ready for the next waypoint, you probably have the timing about right. Keep in mind that every time a team receives a few more weeks to complete one of the steps, they wait until the last week or so at best to bear down. By the time several extensions have been authorized, a three- to four-month, No-Slack Launch will have ballooned to six months, even a year or more.

Big chunks of the No-Slack Launch should place key executives out of their formal positions on the management team. For example, during the Launch sequence, they should be asked to serve as Co-Champions in the development of key initiatives and later to provide company-wide Execution "oversight" on the progress of their assigned initiative. These cross-organizational duties are performed in addition to being responsible as line executives for the achievement in their own department of *all* initiatives.

The No-Slack Launch stands in stark contrast to the counsel that everything must be perfectly prepared before any kind of launch, with troves of analyzed data, a completely articulated strategy and new business model, and all the right people in the right positions. Many leaders who follow that advice find themselves shunted onto the side tracks, still waiting to fire up their engine as old and new competitors and the market roar by and key employees leave to find better vehicles to advance their careers. Preparation is important, but not at the expense of motion. Motion has value in itself because you begin immediately to accrue small victories and generate fresh insights that entice the undecided to make a commitment to come on board.

Pausing up front to make this kind of investment in a well-designed, tightly compressed structure of planning steps, each with all team members aboard and under the lights together, greatly accelerates the experience each member goes through to engage, explore, influence, and align to the new transformation agenda. The leader needs to look for as many opportunities as possible for dialogue among the team members and to structure the leadership forums so that the air time of dominant players is balanced against that available to more thoughtful and less vociferous team members. More about this in the next chapter.

Perhaps the most important reason to get moving is that every day of action accelerates the cycle of organizational learning and adaptation. Leadership teams that have a bias for action and Execution aren't likely to dither at the starting gate. In these cultures, the moment a solution is envisioned, it is put into play. If it proves to be faulty, it is just as quickly jettisoned and harvested for things learned to apply to the ongoing business. This accelerated cycle is at the heart of becoming a strategically agile business that is positioned to disrupt markets rather than be trumped by unexpected and disruptive competitive attacks.

The best way to avoid procrastination during the early Launch steps is to develop a transformation architecture up front that lays out the important waypoints where there will be analysis, input, decisions, plans, and then execution. This architecture has to include all of the critical transformation principles of confronting reality, focus, alignment, engagement, and follow-through. In addition, it must clearly articulate when and where each person in the organization will have a chance to learn, provide input, and then make decisions and commitments that impact his or her area of responsibility. The No-Slack Launch at the front of this roadmap that is embedded in the ACT process is shown in Figure 2.1.

Typically, you should compress the first three steps into no more than a three- to four-month cycle, leaving only two to four weeks between major checkpoints and working sessions. If more time is allowed into the planning process up front, it will begin to weaken the Launch by undermining the sense of urgency, and it won't add quality to get launched and just delays the process of learning.

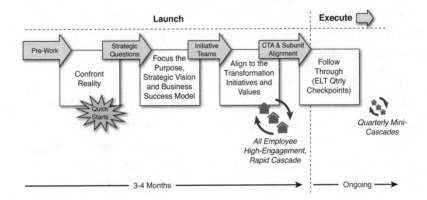

Figure 2.1 The No-Slack Launch

Launch Speed = Simplicity × Compression

The *speed* that runs through all successful transformations is not the kind that should instill concern or fear. It is not the kind of speed that is achieved by omission, or skipping over steps and activities that are on the transformation critical path. Rather, it is on the other side of complexity, where ACT resides. It is the kind of speed that is based on *simplicity* and *compression*. Speed of the "been there, done that" sort. That is made up of many small things such as simplifying the transformation constructs and minimizing the steps, tightly designing key events and decision processes, and cleanly operationalizing the Transformation Initiatives.

One good illustration of the latter is the set of standard templates that all leaders working on the Transformation Initiatives must continue to refine throughout the Launch Phase. This is important to be presented in the Cascade rollout so that all employees can easily grasp their meaning and translate them for relevance and into personal commitments at their level in a single setting. Are you surprised that corporate Transformation Initiatives can and need to be distilled down to the set of a dozen or so slides, as shown in Figure 2.2?

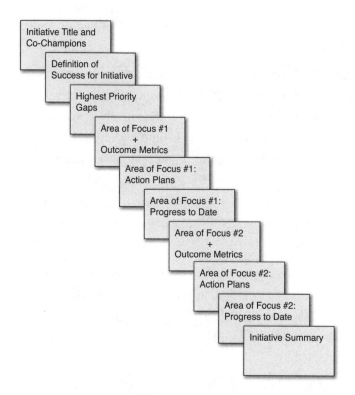

Figure 2.2 Template Set for Transformation Initiatives

Here are some other reasons why speed, simplicity, and compression are important in transformation work.

As the process is launched and the train begins to move, any slack that emerges in the pace can quickly cause a decline in momentum. If too many stretch-outs and reschedules are introduced, forward momentum for the transformation or strategy execution effort can grind to a halt. In fact, it used to be that for convenience, companies would wait until the beginning of a full fiscal or calendar year to launch their efforts. But as the cycle time of everything has decreased, waiting two or three quarters to get launched is no longer an option. Be sure to set the proper pace to move your team and organization through the compressed Launch roadmap you have established to guide the effort.

As the CEO of one of our high-tech transformation clients reflected,

> I've had very few opportunities other than with this process when we've gotten everybody from the CEO all the way through every last person in the organization involved in hearing the same message, aligning goals, and making commitments in such a short time. I think a lot of people completely underestimate the power of getting the entire organization hearing the same simple message and behind a single focus from top to bottom. It was really amazing how much energy was created at one time.

Figure 2.3 reveals a more detailed view of the streamlined transformation architecture you will find useful to launch a transformation. It shows the roadmap that was adapted to support the transformation Launch of a $4 billion global company of about 14,000 employees.

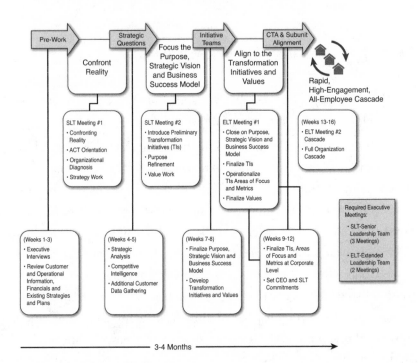

Figure 2.3 The No-Slack Launch Roadmap: A Detailed View

Here's how the roadmap works. First, its streamlined aspect means that all of the planning, launching, and engaging of the three top levels of leaders takes place in just five one-day events: three for the SLT and two for the (ELT), which includes the senior leaders and their direct reports (essentially the leadership teams of the major components of the organization).

The top row of boxes shows the major steps that take place as events in the ACT Launch. The middle row of boxes indicates working sessions for either the SLT or ELT. The bottom row shows the time spans for analysis and planning work. Again, notice that the time spans for this work are only three to four weeks in duration. This company was a fast mover, but even for them there was some concern up front about their ability to keep up with the pace outlined in the roadmap. As they got into it, they proved to be up to the task.

The In-Between Work

One of the major causes of delay in these launch efforts is the time allotted for getting work done between the meetings. We've all been to brainstorming meetings that generated long lists of ideas. But it usually takes a week to get the meeting notes published (if they ever come out). In the absence of structured tablework, a team of administrative support people usually labor for hours to translate scrawling from numerous flip-chart sheets into readable meeting notes. Leaders struggling to push on typically have to review the long lists of random, incomplete, and unprioritized ideas before breaking them into categories and assigning them to interim work teams. A clumsy step like this typically adds at least another week or so of phone calls and lots of prodding and cajoling to get people to open up their schedules to take on the session's follow-on work. Project leaders then have to schedule the first meeting to talk about scope and purpose for their working team. Consequently, another two to three weeks can elapse before the first work session can get scheduled.

At this point, we are four to five weeks out from the Launch meeting, and nothing has happened to advance the thinking and planning. And it will take several more weeks to get the analysis done and the team report prepared for presentation and discussion at the next Launch meeting. By then, you've consumed two months between Launch meetings. Given that you need five scheduled Launch meetings with your SLTs and ELTs, you are in to a minimum eight- to nine-month Launch Phase before anyone below the top three levels of leadership can become fully engaged in your transformation.

How can you effectively collapse the whole Launch process into three to four months? Without losing anything? In fact, while gaining not only precious time but also energy, commitment, and momentum?

First, set the complete timeline with prescheduled dates at the onset of the Launch. That way, everyone knows exactly what needs to be done in terms of decision points at the key working sessions and the analytical work that needs to take place between each main event. This enables your team to envision the full path, much like the speed skier. It will also send a strong signal of your commitment to stay the course for at least the 15–16 months in the typical ACT-cased transformation roadmap. Second, schedule the timing to either avoid or, if necessary, encompass other major corporate events so that you don't swamp people's calendars. If the latter, make sure that the transformation planning portion of your agenda does not receive short shrift.

Devil in the Meeting Details

There has to be a factory-like discipline to the work of executive leaders for a successful, rapid transformation Launch. Each of the five key Launch meetings of your team has to be planned and structured in advance. What advance preparation needs to be done? What is the timed agenda for each convening of the leadership team? Who is presenting what? What specific questions will the tablework teams have to respond to? What worksheets will be developed to guide their deliberations and focus their report outs? What will be the likely next steps leading to the next meeting of the group during Launch? If you get the design right, the meeting will run itself, leaving you as transformation leader the luxury to listen more carefully, better time your inputs, and orchestrate smooth transitions from one difficult decision to the next.

Next, make sure to end each SLT and ELT Launch meeting with a 30- to 60-minute work session to kick off the first meeting of any working teams that have been tasked to complete interim work before the next leadership meeting.

All of these details must be planned well in advance. And to what effect?

When debriefed before closing even the first SLT meeting in an ACT-based Launch Phase, executives always report the meeting broke all company records, and they say that all company meetings should work like that. Their buy-in to your transformation starts right there with SLT Meeting #1.

So make sure that your team knows well in advance when Launch meetings start and end and hold them to the full agenda. Establish a no-cut rule for the leadership team and ban early departures for flights. By not allowing the normal amount of slack to enter the system, you not only speed the cycle time to engage the full organization and shorten the time to generate results, but also engineer a significant shift in the operating rhythm of the company. There will be more of a sense of the value of speed generated through real-time feedback and dialogue, tight frameworks to prioritize discussions and actions, and expedited (or eliminated) administrative tasks. That should give you another insight into how Doing More ON Less works in the game of transformation and strategy planning.

If you don't take charge of the first meeting (step) in your transformation Launch, others certainly will fill the vacuum.

Transformation Initiative Co-Champion Structure

Another somewhat different aspect of the ACT approach is that the core Transformation Initiatives are developed and initially launched by *Co-Champions* drawn from the Senior Leadership Team. They are announced by the CEO at the moment the SLT has coalesced around the three to four corporate-wide Transformation Initiatives, but before they become operationalized into Areas of Focus and Metrics.

Typically, it is said that if more than one person is in charge, then no one is in charge. But in this case, it is different. There are several compelling reasons to go with Co-Champions in rising to a corporate transformation planning challenge. First, it is too easy to ascribe initiatives focused on the market and customers to only the Marketing vice president. Similarly, talent or people engagement initiatives are often given just to the Human Resources vice president to run as some special new program. That leads to business-as-usual programs being launched by functional groups that the operations and field groups might or might not participate in or help drive. While that traditional authority structure may suffice under status quo conditions, it creates neither the robust corporate initiatives nor the company-wide traction during Execution needed for fundamental transformation.

So the ACT-based approach calls for Co-Champions to operationalize each Transformation Initiative during Launch and to continue on to provide "oversight" on progress during the Execution Phase. In fact, it recommends that all members of the SLT be a Co-Champion of one of the initiatives. If not, experience reveals that those not so involved from the onset will not fully understand and be engaged with the corporate Transformation Initiatives. Any senior leadership team members who are given a hall pass during critical transformation meetings will cast very long shadows over their part of the enterprise during the Cascade and throughout the Execution Phase.

Let's consider two very different ways in which a talent Transformation Initiative may be implemented throughout a field organization.

In one example, the corporate transformation game plan has as one of its Transformation Initiatives a talent component, in which field executives opt to rely completely on the Human Resources function to do the work for them. Field executives periodically review and approve programs that Human Resources design. However, it becomes tough for the Human Resources teams to get the time for the reviews, much less create time in the field operations to get their programs implemented. Managers in the field fail to view talent management as a part of their "real" job and don't spend much time on it. The new hiring practices come off as just one more administrative policy guideline. The development program becomes viewed as an optional course to which Field employees are sent only when they have slack time to work on courses for which their part of the organization had little say in the way of design. These poor implementation results may be traced back directly to the lack of accountability and ownership shouldered by line managers to develop and support the talent initiative. Such "siloed" organizations do not view collaboration as essential for success.

Contrast this situation with one in which business and functional departments each have their own commitments to support a corporate Transformation Initiative. Marketing produces more effective campaigns when sales offers input on how customers will respond. Engineering designs better products when Marketing provides customer and competitive analysis to guide the design process. Human Resources is more effective when local line managers actively participate in recruiting top talent. And, Manufacturing has higher quality when partnering early with Engineering so that products are designed to be easy to build from the start. The Co-Champion design initially helps to ensure that the typical gaps due to silos are bridged in the process of operationalizing each company-wide Transformation Initiative and later encourages each business and functional organization to contribute whatever they can to its achievement in an accelerated manner.

The best choices for Co-Champions of company-wide Transformation Initiatives are drawn from the Senior Leadership Team in a manner that results in pairings of functional staff executives with their counterparts in business units, operations, or field groups. These pairs of SLT Co-Champions are responsible for taking the lead on operationalizing their assigned initiative, vetting it in various SLT and ELT meetings along the Launch Phase roadmap, and presenting it in a compelling and consistent (structured) manner for easy employee understanding and commitment/goal setting as part of the Cascade. Later, these Co-Champions are joined by Division Champions to form company-wide Execution "oversight" teams as the process moves beyond the Cascade to the Execution Phase. More about this in Chapter 6.

The typical ACT-based Initiative Co-Champion structure is shown in Figure 2.4. This structure is put in place by the CEO shortly after the transformation roadmap is laid out, and it stays in place throughout the corporate transformation effort, which may involve several years. But during the short Launch Phase, the basic components of this structure consist of five major roles.

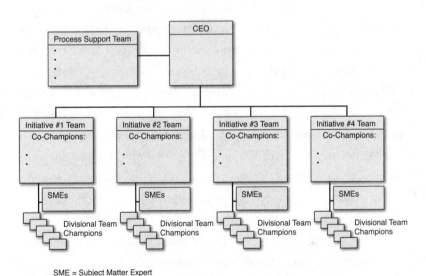

SME = Subject Matter Expert

Figure 2.4 Leading Transformation: Initiative Team Structure

At the top, of course, is the transformation leader; in our enterprise-level transformations, the CEO. His or her role as leader of the corporate transformation is quite straightforward. This is not something that can be delegated. This is an absolute. It is the CEO's role to lay out the transformation roadmap, to create and enforce the "safe passage" environment so essential for high-quality dialogue and decision making, and to guide the leadership team to a corporate transformation game plan that is ready to put into Execution. The CEO must champion the unique ACT-based Cascade process. He or she must also rigorously follow through for performance Execution and value alignment. And the CEO must personally model the company values through his or her visible behaviors and decisions throughout the transformation journey.

Co-Champions drawn from the Senior Leadership Team come next. Their initial job is to adopt a cross-functional perspective on their assigned Transformation Initiative and operationalize it through several compressed rounds of vetting with their peers (SLTs) and with the subunit leadership teams (ELTs) reporting directly to them. Together, the SLT Co-Champions serve with the CEO as the *transformation steering committee*. And in this role, the no-cut policy applies. Like the CEO, they share the burdens of leading the transformation and its Cascade in their own division in an aligned manner and modeling the values through their personal behaviors. As the transformation crosses over from Launch to Execution, the company-wide initiative Co-Champions will be joined by Divisional Champions to form company-wide initiative teams that have Execution "oversight" responsibility. They monitor and report on progress with their company-wide Transformation Initiative and capture and disseminate leading practices on their initiative across the organization on a quarterly basis during Execution.

The CEO and Initiative Co-Champions are supported by the Process Support Team, which consists of the ACT Process Architect and representatives from each of the major process disciplines, that is, leaders in the areas of Human Resources, Training and Development, Performance Management and Compensation, Employee Surveys, and so forth. This team reports directly to the CEO throughout all phases of the ACT-based corporate transformation. We will discuss in more detail the role and makeup of the important Process Support Team in Chapter 9.

It is from the Process Support Team's "cat bird's seat" that the ACT Process Architect guides the alignment of the company's process disciplines to the transformation process and game plan. Here is where the detailed design and logistics for key transformation events spring, as well as where light facilitation of some of the key meetings and Cascade levels comes. But always in the support role. With an ACT-based approach, leaders and line managers and supervisors—not staff professionals or consultants—are in charge of the transformation in all levels of the organization.

Finally, during the Launch Phase the Co-Champions often invite subject matter experts (SMEs), who are content and program management specialists, to help them operationalize their Initiative.

Yes, this is a simple structure for such a huge undertaking. A light saddle for a racehorse comes to mind. That's what we mean by a *leader-led corporate transformation*.

Quick Starts

To put top spin on your transformation Launch, nothing builds early momentum and a sense of urgency like clear progress and early wins.

Just three weeks or so into an ACT-based transformation of a high-flying semiconductor chip company, which had lost its shine, the new CEO gathered his senior team for their first Confronting Reality meeting. They met to review market realities, customer opinions, and the results of confidential interviews with the key leaders of the company. All of those fact sets indicated that there were big problems to fix to get the company back into a high-growth mode.

To distill the most important focus areas, the group worked on an exercise to quickly identify the "really bold ideas" for moving the company forward and the "really stupid things to be avoided." That simple exercise netted out some urgent issues that had long been avoided but that deserved immediate attention. They ranged from the need to launch a new generation of products and reorganizing into profit and loss-oriented divisions to fixing morale and associated high talent turnover.

During a break in the session, the new CEO pulled a small circle of advisors together to contemplate the short lists of dos and don'ts the tablework teams had developed. After the larger group reconvened, most of the executives were expecting him to make some supportive comments about the quality of dialogue and thinking he observed during the previous session before introducing the next work session. In the back of their minds was the multiweek Launch roadmap they had seen in his initial explanation of the process. This led them to expect that the process would take that long to unfold before real decisions would be made to cause action to take place. Not the case for this new CEO.

Instead, the new CEO opened the session by stating that the company appeared to have put itself in a position of being a generation and a half behind on technology. This would require potentially 18 months to two years to rectify. He went on to say that over the next couple of months, many tough decisions about current R&D spending would require more analysis and refinement of the strategy. On the subject of the morale issue, he explained that the leadership team would work through a process over some period of time, first setting values and then living them and gradually restoring confidence in winning throughout the company. Making people feel better on the inside, on the other hand, he reasoned was something that every individual would need to address on his or her own. Raising morale would not be a focus of the transformation effort but would certainly be an expected outcome.

Finally, the new CEO addressed the organization design issues, agreeing with the team that the current design was not allowing leaders to make important decisions about their businesses. As a start-up, the original functional design had worked fine. As a growing public company, however, this structure had become too centrally focused and needed to be changed. He felt that if not addressed right off the bat, the antiquated structure would stifle progress on the transformation itself and the initiatives that would follow. So he targeted restructuring as a *Quick Start*. In his mind, there was no need to have more dialogue or analysis about this obstacle and no reason to wait for the full process to unfold to take action. At that moment, he decided to change the structure and immediately tasked the vice president of Human Resources with initiating the design of the new divisional organization to be implemented immediately.

This decisive action, or Quick Start, sent a clear signal to the team that issues they brought up would be seriously considered for immediate action if warranted—that even the streamlined Launch process would be interrupted and accelerated for cause. It signaled to the team that this was not some overly bureaucratic process that was being followed. When the time was right to make a call and move on, there would be no waiting.

After being established by the executive leader, the Quick Start convention kept members of the leadership team on the edge of their seats for the remainder of their four-month Launch Phase. As a result, the team moved into the next steps in the ACT-based Launch with an acute sense that what they were working on would absolutely have an impact. As the CEO reflected, sometime following this intervention,

> Quick Starts established confidence in the organization that we could win. They were very powerful, and that sent a signal to the team that this was going to be an action-oriented process.

One of the most difficult balances for a leader to strike is wanting to move with speed versus taking the "time" to have deeper dialogue and engage a broader group to enrich the thinking and propagate ownership of the decisions. As you refine the architecture of your transformation process and get the effort launched, look for those major no-brainer issues that are getting in the way of progress, the ones that don't require a lot more analysis to address, and take them on immediately as Quick Starts. People will appreciate your decisiveness and honesty, knowing that their time won't be wasted on a process that might not address the really important issues facing the company. The boost in energy and momentum you will experience will be palpable.

Tips for Structuring Your Transformation Launch

- Be parsimonious in adding extra nice-to-have steps and methodologies to the core ACT roadmap, which is streamlined to enable speed and to avoid increasing complexity and energy-sapping task overload.

- Opt for a No-Slack Launch that runs in parallel to the routine management process, so that the development of your transformation game plan does not receive short shrift.

- Lay out a transformation roadmap that lets everyone know when and how they will become involved.

- Bias your process towards motion, not analysis, to build early support and energy

- Compress your Launch Phase into a 3-4 month cycle.

- Remember that productive speed in transformation comes from simplicity of content and compression of process; not from careless omissions or skipping essential steps.

- Carefully advance plan not only major transformation events, but also the in-between work.

- Avoid having "wallflowers" on the Senior Leadership Team; they will cast large shadows over their part of the organization during the Cascade and Execute Phases.

- Make all SLT members a Co-Champion of a corporate Transformation Initiative during planning and execution "oversight."

- Create a transformation Process Support Team to make sure that all of the enterprise's process disciplines are aligned in support of the corporate transformation game plan.

- Launch *"Quick Starts"* before you complete the corporate transformation game plan.

- Bias all phases of your corporate transformation game plan to be leader-led, not staff professional or consultant led.

Endnotes

1. For more on the subject of organizational "imprinting," refer to Seymour Sarason, *The Creation of Settings and the Future Societies*, Brookline Books, 1972, 1989.

2. Robert H. Miles, "Accelerating Corporate Transformations—Don't Lose Your Nerve!" *Harvard Business Review*, January–February 2010.

3

Crafting Your Launch Process

Easily overlooked by BIG thinkers, but once unleashed in an organization, there is a micro intervention that can profoundly affect the whole of the enterprise and its unfolding transformation. We refer to "it" alternatively as *structured dialogue* or simply, *tablework*. Each, along with a clear transformation game plan and roadmap, as we have discussed, contributes to the creation of safe passage for all involved in the transformation journey.

By *creating safe passage*, we mean develop a corporate transformation game plan along with the rules of engagement. To get the most from his or her Senior Leadership Team, the leader needs to set some ground rules to govern how the team works together to confront reality, explore alternatives, and make decisions.

We use a simple but refined technique called *structured dialogue* in all important Senior Leadership Team (SLT) meetings, starting with the initial Confronting Reality session that kicks off a corporate transformation launch. Such teams are made up of very different individuals—some with lots of power and influence, others with comparatively little. Some hold sway over the most important businesses in the enterprise, while others are trying to get unproven ones off the ground. Some have a surfeit of resources, while others are scratching and angling for every dime. Some have been on the team forever, and others are newcomers from inside or outside the organization. Some majored in finance, others in engineering, others in people, and still others in hard knocks.

Suffice it to say, if you assemble such a diverse team around a boardroom table and conduct a discussion headed toward consequential decisions involving major reallocations of resources like it's a jump ball at a Final Four tournament, you're not likely to get much in the way of a thoughtful outcome. Indeed, half of the assembled team probably won't participate. And most certainly, only the "winners" of the discussion and debate will be committed to the decision they wrested from their peers.

From the onset of transformation planning by the Senior Leadership Team right down through the Cascade sessions in which we bring individual contributors aboard, we deploy this micro intervention to break down problem-solving and decision-making biases and intensively engage all concerned. We embed it so deeply in the way our clients work together that they come to absorb it into the way they lead the transformation and, ultimately, how they manage on a day-to-day basis. And they make it a centerpiece in the way they set up and run the downstream Cascade meetings to engage and enlist all employees.[1]

But we are getting ahead of ourselves.

Let's look at a few common pathologies in organizations that inhibit not just rapid transformation but management in general.

Confronting Today's Reality

Denial is the opium of losers. Nothing guarantees fatal errors faster than seeing only what you want to see. Winning is all about realism, accepting truth, and acting on it quickly and more effectively than your competitors. Seeing things from the market or customer perspective, from the outside-in, that's what matters. History is littered with the defeats of deniers. The challenge is to determine what it takes to leap from perilous denial to positive realism. At the heart of the matter is your realization that the flip side of denial is courage.

Denial takes many forms; one situation illustrates it well. A multi-billion dollar company had just assigned a new CEO and COO. They were hoping to reverse a five-year slide in sales.

Two weeks into the assignment to develop the process architecture for helping the company speed its transformation and strategy execution process, a small team had been given an office on the executive floor to conduct their work. The office had all the appearances of having been hastily vacated. There were still files in the drawers and a large map on the wall, with pins placed on once-promised but long forgotten projects. While cleaning out the files, the team noticed a document right on the top of a stack in one of the drawers. Titled "Strategic Options," the file was authored by one of the world's leading strategy consulting firms. It was dated two years prior to the team's arrival, and although aspects of the game had changed, it was still worth a look as part of the up-front discovery process.

Flipping past the first few pages, the team stopped at a page titled "Executive Summary Recommendations." There in front of them, with some items circled in red, were all in plain view the straight-up, harsh realities that needed to be addressed currently—only the report had been written and submitted to the previous CEO two years earlier.

The current executive leaders welcomed the team with hopeful comments about the ability to tee up the "real issues" that for so long had been taboo. The prior CEO clearly had access to the report and presumably had reviewed its recommendations. He just hadn't acted on any of them. In contrast, the new CEO and COO were very motivated to confront the realities surrounding the business they had inherited and were quick to put these data on the agenda for executive discussion. This recurrent story of strategies stored as binders on shelves or files in drawers is all too common and a clear reminder that many of the issues are typically right there in plain sight but are simply not confronted and addressed.

About the Emperor's Clothes

It is critical for leaders to set a tone that allows the team to confront reality. You would be amazed at how many people are trapped in the "Emperor Has No Clothes" syndrome. Even at the executive levels, certain taboo topics become routinely avoided. There is often a lot of pent-up energy to let out the truth. Surprisingly, it often takes just a bit of structured dialogue (the creation of a safe place to speak openly) and the guidance from the leader for a team to begin driving hard at the real roadblocks to progress. It is a fool's game to try to suppress the real issues. Everyone knows the problems exist whether they speak openly about them or not. People whisper in the halls or joke over drinks after work about these issues. But until safe passage is provided, most people will not risk mentioning anything about them in front of the boss. If it is not clear how the issues will be accepted or if anything will be done about them, there is only risk for speaking up with no clear benefit.

Sometimes, more than simple dialogue and executive encouragement is needed to suspend taboo status. It often takes a little shock to the system to unlock the conversation, which can come from any level of management. At the worst-performing division of a global industrial products business, the team had spent a day and a half denying that they had any problems. Then, one exasperated and brave manager came back from a lunch break and broke the logjam by playing over the sound system the country song, "Pissin' in the Wind." His colleagues immediately realized that what they had been doing all morning amounted to about the same thing. This is not necessarily a best-practice recommendation for everyone, but sometimes one brave soul needs to step up and call the team out onto the ice. More often that will need to be you as a team member and sometimes as the leader.

Encouraging conversations that are critical of the company and leadership to be handled out in the open allows problems to be addressed sooner and new ideas to surface. To suppress these conversations does not make the issues go away; it just drives people into a quiet mode of resentment and cynicism. None of those behaviors are useful when looking to constructively confront reality. The ability for leaders to take constructive criticism is the starting point, and that means letting your team tell you, the Emperor, what they need to about your clothes.

Dialogue Versus Discussion

Over two thousand years ago, Plato got it right when he observed that truth emerges only through dialogue. Socrates soon followed with a general appeal for more time spent through discourse or conversation to get to the bottom of human affairs.

There can be no real understanding, commitment, or, ultimately, engagement in the absence of dialogue. That's why structured dialogue needs to be a core element in leading a transformation or gaining commitment to execute a strategy.

A critical distinction in conversations that most of us are typically unconscious of on a daily basis is the difference between *dialogue* and *discussion*. They are quite different modes of having a conversation. At the core, the purpose of having a dialogue is to search for deeper meaning and understanding. The essence of discussion is to net out differing opinions to get to a final answer. Both are necessary at different times and situations.

The Latin roots of the word *discussion* come from the same place as the words *percussion* or *concussion* and have to do with opposing views being batted back and forth. You know you are in the mode of discussion when, in the midst of a full meeting, two people begin to lock into a rapid back-and-forth with a lot of bystanders to their banter. Discussion is occurring when people are jockeying for airtime, working to have the winning idea, advocating positions, or arguing key points and assumptions. If someone else is speaking and you are trying to break in by saying, "Yes, but..., right, but just think about, let me make a point...," then you are definitely in discussion mode. Or even if you are not speaking up but your mind is conjuring up a rebuttal while the other person is still talking, you're in discussion mode.

Typically, as businesspeople, we will naturally be in discussion mode most of the time. We have all been trained well to debate points, make convincing arguments, and influence others when a decision is due. Discussions are useful in getting to an answer or making a final decision. But discussions are not necessarily useful in generating deep understanding of reality or generating innovative ideas for growth— which are essentials at the beginning of a transformation.

Dialogue, on the other hand, is a form of conversation that is more focused on working to get a deeper understanding and discovering new possibilities within the whole situation. It is about asking the right questions, not coming up with the right answers. Dialogue is often marked by short periods of silence while people are thinking through and internally integrating what has been said. There is no fight for airtime. You are more likely to hear questions such as, "Tell me what you mean by that," or "If we went with that, how would that change things?" As you listen to someone talking, if you are working to internalize what they are saying and integrate it into your thinking and mindset and building on or adding to their ideas, you are likely in a mode of dialogue.

To be clear, dialogue is not about "feel good" or "self-affirming" conversations, but rather is a tool for getting at tough truths about the business. A partner in a private equity firm describes the value of dialogue well:

> The dialogue is where the answers come from. People don't necessarily answer the (due diligence) questions correctly in the beginning, but through the dialogue we collectively arrive at the right answers. Getting to the right allocations and profit models doesn't come from looking at spreadsheets but

by really thinking about how the business actually operates. Once the right numbers are brought together and match reality, management easily comes to the same logical conclusions and they make the decisions.

A critical element of truly engaging your team to confront reality is to know how to structure and hold a dialogue, a subject we take up shortly. When done correctly, dialogues end up as very powerful work sessions because they are carefully structured to facilitate everyone's initial input, make it safe to engage in courageous conversations, and more often than not generate breakthrough ideas.

Generating Dialogue as a Leader

Sometimes even when leaders feel they have a real knack for open conversations with their teams, they still overpower others with their styles. For example, one CEO had a penchant for engaging in debate. Debate was his way of getting his team to engage on a topic, to explore different perspectives, and to finally come up with a quality decision. He was quite strong at debating and had more experience at a higher level than anybody else in the room; plus he was competitive. So he could usually win a debate. Those are all positive traits, but when he was looking to establish an open dialogue with his team, the end result was that few, if any, people were willing to take him on in a debate. Controversial topics were avoided, and there was no true confrontation of reality. Even so, the CEO left those forums wishing that more people had joined in and argued more vigorously. He wanted more of their active participation.

After one session in which he effectively parried several concerns about the current business model based on external data sources that might have been a little dated or that had modeled the environment differently than he would, the team became very quiet. The gremlins of denial were rearing their ugly heads again! At a break during the session, he was told about this dynamic and realized that what he really wanted was for the team to come to grips with some new market realities and to engage in an open dialogue about their implications. All of that was necessary to begin sharpening the strategy, business model, and culture of the company. But he also realized that his debate-oriented efforts to get them to talk more were having the reverse effect.

After the break, the CEO shared his personal perspective on the data. He explained that he had a natural tendency to debate simply for the sake of argument. He pointed out that he actually believed the conclusions in the studies and had recognized for some time that the company's competitive differentiation had faded. He said,

> Look, we can debate and drill down on these data for months. But the reality is that they will still tell us the same things. It's not necessarily what we want to hear, but we know it's true enough that we need to get on with creating new strategies. Given that things have changed a lot since our heydays, what do you think we need to do?

The CEO's shift from a debate posture to one of personal sharing and invitation immediately opened up the dialogue in the room. The leaders seeking the change now had executive airtime to elaborate on what had been said and point out their views about market shifts that had occurred and where the company needed to change. The fence-sitters now saw that it was time to get off the fence and engage in discussions that were critical to the business. And, we'd be lying if we said that there were no skeptics remaining in the room. But, it was also clear to them that it was time to deal with the truth and move on.

When you're the leader, your answers, especially if provided too early, always get to be the right ones—at least for that moment. You will win every debate and can dominate every discussion. But by knowing when to step back to let your team dialogue to get to the truth, you will unlock a powerful transformation tool that is essential to confronting reality.

Priming the Pump

Often, leadership teams as well as entire companies fall into the rut of accepting too many "givens" about their business and the way they operate.

- "They don't want to hear the truth, so why beat your head against a wall."
- "They've got some sort of agenda, and, hey, I just work here!"
- "Sure, there are tough problems, but that's why they get paid the big bucks to solve them."

You have probably heard or even made comments like these along the way during your career. But who are people talking about? Who makes up the "they" group? Almost invariably, the "theys" are those in charge and in control of everything. "They" also sometimes represents the whole system of management in an organization. At an extreme, people imagine it is the "Man," the power brokers, the oppressors, and, most certainly, a different and separate group from the "real" workers. This kind of thinking sets up a victim mentality among those who rationalize that it is simply their job to toil under illogical and unfair rules that others have set. In any event, this "they" sort of thinking amounts to a mighty roadblock to transforming a company or a major part of it.

These "we" and "they" distinctions, once established at the top, replicate themselves all the way down the hierarchy. This separation causes authentic communications to break down and creates pent-up frustrations as critical issues fail to be addressed. As each layer of managers holds back the realities just a bit from their bosses, a profound sense of false reality begins to flourish at the top. Such an executive disconnect with the business reality freezes innovative thinking throughout the enterprise and inhibits transformation often when needed the most.

How can you unlock the truth to start your transformation with a sharp sense of reality?

The best way to make it safe for people to criticize the status quo is to start with a strictly confidential round of interviews with the SLT conducted by an objective third party. Many leaders will say up-front things like, "On my team we all know each other really well; nobody is shy for sure, so we can just open things up with each other in the meeting. So I'm not sure we'll learn anything new from the interviews."

This perspective is very common. Most of the time, the interviews reveal that overall the leaders are right about many of the key points. However, the common interview experience creates a feeling that the team owns the issues themselves. More important, most leaders are not perfectly well rounded. Each has his or her own "flat sides," which often become visible and discussable for the first time when strictly confidential interview results are reported out by a third party to jumpstart the "real" discussion. This approach simultaneously enables leaders to get to know themselves better while making it safer for their employees to enter into more authentic dialogue about real issues. Although these confidential interviews are designed to be brief, they are organized into three topics: (1) gauging the magnitude of change that will be required by the transformation, (2) assessing what parts of the organization require the most improvement—the "Gaps," and (3) evaluating the functioning of the SLT and what it needs from its leader. These findings are factored into the early Confronting Reality exercise that helps focus the transformation game plan.

Canary in a Coal Mine

In addition to the accountability of leaders to openly confront reality up front, there is an equal accountability for the people at all levels to rise to this challenge throughout a transformation. Being included for input into strategic planning and execution is not a passive right to be "in the know." It is an active role that requires risk taking to engage and an accountability to provide constructive input and ideas for solutions.

A year into the transformation launch at a large high-tech semiconductor manufacturer, a team of middle managers was convened to evaluate how the effort was going. The team was given several weeks to deliberate and tasked to deliver what its members thought were the biggest obstacles at one of the quarterly leadership meetings.[2]

Most of the executives other than the new CEO were refugees from the company's failed old guard. It was the perception among middle managers that many of these company leaders were attempting to solve current corporate challenges the old way, with reactive restructurings, crisis management, and top-down decision making. They believed many senior executives were not making difficult decisions and sticking with them. Therefore, heading the list of major obstacles to transformation was the very thorny issue of lack of trust and credibility of top management.

When their work was completed, the major challenge to the team had just begun: how to constructively confront their bosses with their major findings and then to work with them to find solutions that could be put into action.

The members of the team felt quite responsible for their task. As one explained, "We now have 400 middle managers who are committed to the change process, and we're afraid of losing momentum."

The ground had been softened by having the senior executives get prepared to receive some hard feedback. The night before the middle manager presentation, the executives explored what was at stake with this intervention, how difficult it might be for their subordinates to speak candidly about the problems on their watch, how to avoid defensive responses to tough feedback, and what next steps they should be prepared to take in doing something constructive about what they learned.

The next morning, the tension was broken by the leader of the middle manager team, when he began the presentation by saying,

I feel like a canary going in to test the safety of a mine! (Audience laughter.) If my wings are still flapping after a few minutes, the folks with the real messages will come forward to present their parts of the middle manager feedback.

He apologized in advance for focusing on the negatives that would follow but explained that his team felt that the executive leaders in the room had a duty to deal with the issues being brought forth. He also explained that the team represented all the company's middle managers, and they had promised to deliver feedback to them following the meeting.

At center stage during the presentation was the trust and credibility challenge to the old executive guard. The essence of the challenge to senior leaders was that they were being perceived as risk avoiders who were paying only lip service to the transformation effort. Empowered middle managers, who had left the initial high-engagement Cascade experience, understanding the need for transformation and having committed to specific actions to support it, had been repeatedly frustrated when they approached their bosses with improvement recommendations.

To help with this important reality confrontation, the encounter was tightly structured. The middle management team was coached to leave emotions at the doorstep of the leadership meeting and to buttress the obstacles they identified with hard facts. They were also counseled about avoiding defensive responses and encouraged to ask executives to only pose questions for clarification during the presentation. Later, they would work on their own to come up with initial responses to the main obstacles.

After the session closed, middle managers were invited to stay overnight while senior executives worked into the evening to develop a response to each obstacle. They prefaced their report with the key obstacles to middle managers the next morning with a proclamation they had crafted the night before. It read as follows:

> The members of this group strongly condemn and disown any action or threat made toward any employee for constructively speaking their mind. Should this have occurred, or occur in the future, we strongly urge that individual to go immediately to the Ombudsman. We value open and honest communication.

When the senior executive presentation was completed, the assembled group of executives and managers worked to identify the five most critical obstacles to the company's transformation effort, and then five teams, each a mixture of senior and middle managers, were formed, assigned an obstacle, and instructed to identify the most important action steps that needed to be taken to remove it. Throughout the process, the CEO created a safe setting for this important confrontation of reality, and he placed the recommendations of these joint teams on the critical path of the second year of the company's transformation effort.

It was by thoroughly thinking through these process steps that the executives were able to effectively confront the reality of the transformation they had been leading and make substantive and timely midcourse corrections. A year later, the company was featured in the *San Francisco Chronicle* as "Silicon Valley's *Comeback Company of the Year*."

The most important outcome of this critical step of confronting reality is providing safe passage that enables a group of leaders to rapidly work through facts and come to grips with the sobering and simple truths. There are time-tested ways of giving lower-level employees the confidence and courage to come out of the shadows to constructively confront higher-ups when they think someone or something is out of line. This is as true both for VPs reporting to the CEO as it is for front-line employees addressing individual contributors.

Constructing a simple framework for dialogue, which you'll see more about in the description of Cascades, and planning all the details of this type of engagement with your team are critical. The reason being—if the canary's wings stop flapping as the first brave soul raises concerns and is ignored or chastised, nobody else will follow him into the conversation.

How Tablework and Structured Dialogue Work

Following countless applications across different industries, organization types, and global cultures, a seemingly simple and mundane but very powerful vehicle for consistently generating high-quality dialogue has emerged. For simplicity, let's just call it *tablework*. Here's how tablework exercises work.

First, most meetings begin with a transfer of information before participants dig in to make sense of it and hopefully translate it into a decision that will be put into action or referred for further study. By now you get the sense that in an ACT-guided environment, considerable preparation would have been devoted to making this presentation material as simple and compelling as possible. Having said that, the first rule in tablework is, after receiving the presentation, allow only questions for clarification. Don't let anyone jump the gun with their first ideas or pet responses or fire volleys back and forth across the boardroom table before the presenter takes a seat.

Second, shortly after responding briefly to those, and only those qualifying questions, you must disaggregate the group before later reconvening them for dialogue and decision making in the general forum. If the group is relatively small, such as an assembly of the Senior Leadership Team, after the factual presentation, break the attendees into three- to four-person tablework teams that literally meet around the corners of the conference table. Make sure to break the assembled group down into tablework teams. A larger group is broken down into smaller groups of no more than six to seven people seated at round tables. The reason for this number is that if you have more people per dialogue group, there will not be enough airtime for everyone to participate in a reasonable time frame. And please note that in either case, no one leaves the room. Tablework teams are not breakout teams, who have to depart the scene in search of remote places to meet and who waste precious time with their comings and goings. It was breakout teams that we believe gave rise to the notion of "herding cats." Even for large gatherings of executives, we recommend setting up a large ballroom at a hotel, full of round tables, each buzzing in dialogue on the same question. Such gatherings can accommodate hundreds of people sorted into dozens of tablework teams at round tables, where their work together can be intimate, efficient, and engaging.

The third rule is to have very clear instructions and a simple output template to address each specific question. Fourth, the time needs to be fixed and relatively constrained for each question to drive for clarity and the appropriate level of analysis and decision making within the group. Every tablework group that experiences successful dialogue always mentions that it would be nice to have had more time. But every work group that tries to leave the time open-ended only generates an overthinking of the issues and generates longer, unprioritized lists than are required. Dialogue by its nature is intended to create expansive conversations about a topic, so if you start without a tight structure of scope, timing, and specific answer formats, the conversation will drift all over the place and generate no useful conclusions. So keep it focused and time-bound.

With clear instructions in hand, the tablework starts with each person taking a few minutes to think of his or her own response. This quiet time at the beginning is essential in that it allows the internal thinkers a chance to process the questions before the extroverted talkers start generating active conversation. During this initial quiet time, each person writes his or her answers down on a worksheet.

This simple, initial reflective task forces each group member to engage with the subject matter and arrive at preliminary ideas before the conversation starts. This helps clarify people's thoughts before active dialogue begins, helps to avoid rambling speeches, and encourages everyone—not just the most vocal—to become more emboldened to share answers that might appear to be too controversial or unrealistic before real dialogue begins in earnest.

Next, during tablework each person is invited to share his or her best answer or two with his or her table group. At this point, again, it is important to follow first with questions for clarification from others. This is a time to get ideas out in the open, not to edit or judge them. Each team member should be given an opportunity to give his or her first idea before anyone is permitted to give their second idea. It allows people of lower organizational standing or less forceful personalities to be fully heard. Oftentimes, the best new ideas come from unexpected people.

To make sure the tablework team follows this routine, three roles are assigned before the process begins. One of the tablework participants serves as a *Recorder*, who is responsible for capturing all the ideas and ultimately prioritizing them on a structured worksheet. This structure also keeps tablework "bullies" from shutting down other points of view before they are fully shared, typically with comments like, "You know, in the field it really isn't like that..." or "Technically, you're right, but it will never work because...." In addition, a *Facilitator* and a *Presenter* are identified by the team members. The appointed Facilitator leads the discussion at the table to select the best answers to share with the larger meeting group and keeps the process on track and on time. When the task is completed, the Recorder notes the final answers on a worksheet, and the Presenter, who has been organizing his or her thoughts during the group's deliberations, will stand up and share the opinions and recommendations that have been summarized on the team's worksheet.

Each tablework team will have generated dialogue and then prioritized, weeded, and captured the best ideas. Multiply that by every tablework team. As readouts are done in the presence of the larger group, typically common threads emerge. It is easy to see where consensus exists and where there is disagreement; where inferences and assumptions are clear or specifically where they require further study. This structure of readouts also protects the individuals from any worry about putting forth controversial topics as they are reporting on the team's work, not just voicing their opinions. A majority of people, despite what individuals tell you as a leader, have difficulty telling the leaders in a constructive way that they do not agree with them. The readouts allow that to happen in a nonthreatening and predictable way. In this manner of structured dialogue, the leader can establish open dialogue and streamline decision making; both of which are important elements for creating "safe passage" in a transformation planning process.

What arguably is quite simplistic is also a powerful method for rapidly engaging an entire organization with a leader-led approach. An executive who has led both Business Sales and Human Resources departments in back-to-back appointments at a multibillion dollar company underscored a critical aspect of the tablework process when he said to us,

> Simplicity has to be a part of this. The agendas, meeting designs, and even the questions asked need to be simple. This lets the people focus on doing the thinking rather than running through a complex program. The value is in the discussions with each other. And when it is simple enough, people all the way down to the front lines can use the same tools and meeting designs to lead their teams.

The only remaining step in the tablework process is to close the loop on how leaders will accept the input from the group. This is an important step. Participants in a tablework dialogue will want to know that their feedback was heard and is being genuinely considered. There is a temptation for many leaders to process the feedback immediately and come to conclusions and answers on the spot. But that can undermine the idea that full consideration will be made of the ideas. Everyone knows when a forgone conclusion is rolled out for supposed feedback. That will certainly be received worse than not asking for feedback at all. And to be clear, not every decision needs to be opened for dialogue at all levels.

To close well, the process requires that the leader share his or her observations about the quality of the dialogue and the ideas that have been presented. The worksheets from each tablework group should be collected for further analysis. Note that there is no need to collect every individual's worksheet; that just creates an overload of items the group has already weeded out and defeats the purpose of providing "safe passage" for participants for some of their important but controversial ideas. Notice also that nothing has been mentioned about the ubiquitous use of "flip charts," which often accompany group work. They are banished from tablework activities in favor of simply structured team worksheets, which are used to channel consistent analyses and presentations and studied after the event. We have also taken to using collaborative wisdom-of-the-crowd software solutions to allow table groups to input their answers and have them instantly captured and presented along with those of their fellow table groups. The advantage of the software solutions is that those same ideas can be immediately ranked and rated for prioritization, with all of that information captured and presented back in real time.

Finally, a commitment needs to be made by the leader that the feedback received will shape the thinking in the revised plans and commitments. Indeed, before the group breaks up, the leader should announce the future milestones in the process and when people can expect to hear the final outcomes. Other output from the meeting will require future study, and these assignments and delivery dates must be communicated before the event closes. This results in real work in real time with concrete outcomes and next steps, which most meetings cannot promise. If you have already come to a full conclusion and don't want to change your mind on a particular topic, don't open a dialogue about it.

Top strategy development is handled primarily by the senior executives, but it should be opened for dialogue with the middle management team for a reality check and input. So when you design your timeline for engaging the organization in a strategy execution or transformation effort, be sure to build in the appropriate but always compressed cycle for dialogue before the final decisions need to be made. This method of tablework—which gets everyone's ideas out on the table before requiring everyone to narrow the choices down to those that can have the greatest potential for impact—puts power in the hands of leaders at every level in the organization to engage their direct team in dialogue, idea generation, decision making, and ultimately, commitment setting. By simplifying the method for doing this, leaders at all levels are able to transfer active championing of the required breakthrough thinking, passion, and performance to their own teams. This is what we mean by a leader-led transformation.

In many conventional management approaches, as illustrated in Figure 3.1, lower-level leaders are only expected to play passive roles: They are simply asked to be the conduit of messages and expectations from above and make the changes they are told to implement in their workgroups. Passive participation, such as simply allowing or enabling changes, results in a compliance culture that is relegated to status quo or incremental improvement aspirations. But by establishing the set of process guidelines of safe passage and structured dialogue, you empower and equip your leaders at all levels to be proactive in exploring with their people innovative ways to drive your corporate transformation agenda.

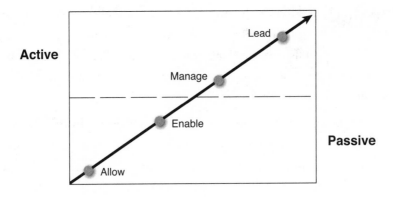

Figure 3.1 Passive Versus Active Leadership

Creating Safe Passage

The other underlying process dimension in leading corporate transformations is "creating safe passage." We first introduced this concept in Chapter 1, "Accelerated Corporate Transformation: The Foundations," along with the need to establish and communicate to all involved from the get-go a transformation roadmap to let everyone understand the scope of the transformation game plan and senior leadership's commitment to launching and sustaining it. Such a roadmap importantly lets everyone know how and when they will become involved in the process. Just publishing such a roadmap commits leaders to see its course through, which initially is laid out for a minimum of 18 months from the time the transformation gauntlet is laid down.

And, as we have also seen in this chapter on underlying processes, another way to set this stage for safe passage is through carefully designed meetings based on tablework principles. Rather than school executives in the whats and wherefores of creating safe passage, we deploy the simple tablework intervention for putting it into practice, starting at the SLT level. The essence of safe passage comes from the manner in which we structure dialogue in all meetings having to do with important transformation issues and decisions.

Once structured dialogue is routinely seeded into the transformation launch meetings, senior executives become accustomed to running meetings and making decisions in that manner. Then they take structured dialogue to important meetings with their own leadership teams, and so on, until the tablework approach it entails becomes the way in which managers and employees at all levels engage with the transformation game plan and set their personal commitments to action to support it. It is the way the Cascade to all managers and employees is conducted by immediate supervisors at each level and every department in the enterprise. As one division president of an oil and gas services company put it,

> This process has shown me how to lead from the back of the room. And what is amazing is that by letting my team dialogue, they are coming up with their own tough decisions, and for the most part all I need to do is agree and help them with resources. That is so much easier and effective than driving it all myself.

The key steps that you need to take to ensure "safe passage" are summarizerd in Figure 3.2.

By throwing all of these process levers, in a matter of a few months, not over a period of years, safe passage and structured dialogue leaven the culture and management process throughout the enterprise.

Throughout the rest of the book, you'll see how a carefully refined corporate transformation plan can be deployed to run fast, drive decisive action through leaders at all levels, productively engage the full organization, and achieve breakthrough results—quickly. In our experience, the only way to create the enormously productive feelings of engagement and safe passage is to kick off your transformation or strategy execution effort by showing the organization a well-thought-out roadmap that is simple, makes sense, is market-focused, reveals where and how people at all levels will be truly engaged, and doesn't sugarcoat the seriousness of decisions to be made. With sound structure and process in place, you will have a foundation for speed and safe passage, the keys to a great transformation Launch.

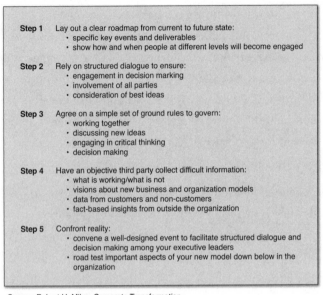

Source: Robert H. Miles, Corporate Transformation
Resources: Reprinted by permission.

Figure 3.2 Key Steps in Creating "Safe Passage"

Tips for Crafting Your Transformation Launch Process

- Make sure to start your transformation Launch Phase by *"creating safe passage;"* don't send any canaries into your coal mine!

- Incorporate *"structured dialogue"* and *"tablework"* into every corporate transformation event.

- Understand the difference between *"dialogue"* and *"discussion"* and when and how to employ them.

- Use these process principles from your first transformation meeting with the Senior Leadership Team all the way down to every transformation meeting between your supervisors and employees.

- And remember, dialogue and tablework actually speed your corporate transformation process rather than slow down its progress.

Endnotes

1. Robert H. Miles, *Leading Corporate Transformation: A Blueprint for Business Renewal*. San Francisco: Jossey-Bass Publishers, Inc., a Division of John Wiley & Sons, 1997.

2. Robert H. Miles, *Corporate Comeback: The Renewal and Transformation of National Semiconductor*. San Francisco: Jossey-Bass Publishers, Inc., a Division of John Wiley & Sons, 1997, pp. 247–248. Reprinted with permission of the author.

4

The Focus Phase

The second major step in the launch of a corporate transformation is the Focus Phase. In this phase successful transformation leaders must work with their executive team to distill out of the purpose and clear strategic vision developed in the Confronting Reality Phase a limited set of coordinated, enterprise-wide initiatives that form the tracks along which the corporate transformation game plan will proceed. The executive team, working together under mutually agreed-upon ground rules and process architecture, must create what we call the *Transformation Arrow*, a plan-on-a-page that contains the core transformation constructs to which all components and employees of the organization will align.

But before we outline how best to do this, it is important to understand why the Transformation Arrow is so important. It must articulate a new state to which the organization desires to move. It needs to serve as the burning ambition to deliver new value to customers, a better environment for employees, and greater value for shareholders and stakeholders. It is not simply a new set of loosely assembled, uncoordinated initiatives that are pancaked on those already operating in the enterprise.

Let's briefly review the challenges of the Gridlock inhibitor to transformation before we lay out its antidote.

Gridlock and the Task Overload Epidemic

So much needless complexity has been created in today's businesses that much of what people are assigned to do could be left undone without damage to the bottom line. Organizations are running on extreme task overload. And, in reality, only a critical few initiatives have the potential for making a big difference. A majority of items on everyone's to-do lists never get fully attended to anyway.

People and resources have to be more focused on the highest impact areas only. Those Areas of Focus that can contribute the earliest results and the most to the shift in strategic direction must receive an immediate, unfairly generous share of the available resources. Meanwhile, employees need to keep a steady strain on all the other routine things that involve ongoing incremental improvements as part of their job performance.

In the good name of tuning up core processes to drive efficiency, form has overtaken function in many organizations. People scorecard everything that moves, launch multiple process-change initiatives in every business function simultaneously, and demand that everything is a priority where "failure is not an option!" Caught in the clutches of organizational attention deficit disorder, these organizations need the simplicity of a well-conceived, well-orchestrated corporate transformation.

Gridlock typically starts simply, innocuously. First, the Finance department wanted to put new expense management tools and processes in place to better control overhead costs and comply with regulations. That made sense. Then Human Resources launched a new employee performance system so the organization could better identify the top contributors and work to retain and develop them. Marketing initiated a campaign to help boost sales of newly launched products. Manufacturing launched a Six Sigma program that eventually touched marketing, sales, and finance. And the top executive team embarked on a culture-change effort to boost morale. Ironically, the root cause for low morale was likely that too many initiatives were overloading the system and the people. Individually, all of these projects make sense and taken individually are not necessarily bad or excessive. But when launched simultaneously and not aligned and prioritized based on a common strategy, the multiple layers of activity can easily overwhelm an organization, creating Gridlock.

Best Intentions in Big Box Retail

The vice president of Field Operations at one major "big box" retailer provides a good illustration of how Gridlock unfolds under the best of intentions. His organization was buried under the crush of administrative work and tactical rollouts. The company was trying to standardize and improve customer experiences across its entire chain of stores. It had focused on some key initiatives at the top but hadn't fully aligned all of the various programs across functional groups. Each department in the corporate headquarters had a backlog of what they believed to be critically important programs to be rolled out to the field. There were new compensation plans from HR, special sales incentive programs from merchandising, customer service guidelines from marketing, strategy communications and product training from vendors, just to name a few. The functional leaders looking to roll out their programs were quite frustrated with the lack of execution in the field on their programs.

One morning as the senior executive team gathered at headquarters, the Field Operations VP brought in a huge box of papers and put it on the conference table. People were surprised and curious about the box. Then he went on to explain that the box contained printouts and copies of every communication from headquarters that had been sent to the field to be rolled out—during just one month! It was immediately clear that there was no way that field managers could execute all of the actions requested in each email, memo, newsletter, "meeting-in-a-box," employee communication, and so forth. The field managers had no choice but to selectively implement programs based on their own judgment. The result was a lack of full execution of any of the programs in any given geography and very uneven customer experiences across stores—the very thing the programs were intended to "fix."

As a consequence of the Gridlock imposed from all the best intentions from above, a Field Operations manager revealed the unwritten "two-drawer" method that he and his colleagues had devised for keeping up with all of the corporate initiatives. This widespread survival technique involved taking all new memos received in the field regarding corporate initiatives and putting them in a desk drawer. If anyone followed up on a particular memo, it was pulled out of the drawer, considered a "real" priority, and tagged for some sort of action. At the end of the month, if nobody called on the rest of the memos, the stack of memos was moved to a second drawer. After two months, if nobody called to follow up about any of those memos in the second drawer, it was okay to throw those memos away. At the end of each month, the rolling two-month file ultimately got thrown away.

The Field Operations manager swore that after years of following the two-drawer method, only once or twice per month would there be any follow-up from above whatsoever! Instead of spending his day reading and sorting through corporate memos, the manager was able to spend most of his time working in the field, which he thought was more important.

Regardless of the coping method that emerges informally in a gridlocked organization, the message is clear. The need to focus—for simplicity—is a tough idea to get across to a team of leaders, each of whom is trying to drive his or her own major programs. The simple fact remains: You can launch as many initiatives as you want, but the capacity to execute will become a choke point in reaching results if your corporate initiatives are not sorted, prioritized, and sequenced.

Undermining Accountability and Customer Loyalty

Why is this overload and complexity so detrimental?

If there is no clear focus on what is important and too much is happening at once, people who don't deliver results in one area simply point to the other areas where they have gotten the job done. However, the things they accomplished might have been the lowest priorities for the company. Or, worse yet, they rapidly work to "check the box" beside each of their many assigned tasks so at least they can say they did something about everything with which they were charged, focusing on task accomplishment rather than true business impact.

In addition, Gridlock often undermines customer loyalty. Customers come to depend on companies because of their core competencies—Volvo for safety, Nordstrom for customer service, Nike for sports performance, Honda for reliable motors. Does that mean that Volvo doesn't have any performance engineering or pay any attention to ergonomics for comfort? Of course not. But when Volvo advertises, they emphasize safety. When they make trade-offs and tough decisions on manufacturing costs and designs, they bias decisions toward the value of safety.

Nonaligned companies, in contrast, have no central strategic and market focus and end up taking a stand on everything and, therefore, nothing. Such unfocused companies will often launch best-practice initiatives in every part of the business, regardless of whether the area is a differentiator in the eyes of customers. In contrast, a well-focused company drives to achieve best practices in the areas that are the highest value to its customers—ones that galvanize lasting customer relationships.

Busting Through Gridlock

The only way to cure the gridlocked organization and generate the required focus to execute is to be willing to start at the top and set clear direction and priorities to engage and align people's underlying motivations. This is when innovation begins to emerge and build momentum. It takes a leader seeing the pattern of Gridlock and stepping up to prioritize efforts and set a clear direction to get started.

A common fear of many leaders is that if they admit that the organization is doing too much, they will lose their ability to motivate the team to do more. When such leaders keep raising the bar or keep piling on new initiatives, relentlessly, it becomes political suicide for a team member to throw up the white flag and call out the issue of task overload. Instead, everyone just hunkers down further, scrambling for ways to check the boxes on their task lists as fast as they can.

The Leader's Challenge: "Doing More ON Less"

Focus is not about doing less work overall, but rather doing more *on* fewer things. You need not give up on the call for transformational improvements in the organization and its businesses. You just have to be willing to shoulder the risks of clearly articulating a tight focus on what will and won't be done to get there. You need to lead the way by making tough choices, less hedging of bets, and then trust the team to execute with more impact and accountability because they are now called on to drive further against fewer goals.

One of the most damaging business catchphrases in recent history has been "doing more with less." This has become an excuse to reduce resource levels without having the guts to narrow the focus. What you need to demonstrate in your own choices and in what you expect of others is *"doing more ON less"*—focusing everyone on the critical few activities that will provide the greatest impact.

Sharpening the Transformation Arrow

Company leaders will often state up front that they already have a strategy. On the flip side, a survey of over 11,000 employees revealed that only 48% understand the organizational strategy and goals, and only 53% feel that they are focused on the organization's goals. Is it any wonder that company leaders are frustrated that their corporate transformation agendas are not being implemented?[1]

When leaders attempt to launch a corporate transformation, why are their directions not clear enough, and hence, not broadly understood enough to effectively drive action even at the senior management levels? As a starting point, the strategies themselves are often ambiguous, overly complex, and too lofty. They simply aren't taken to a granular enough level to be translated into operational plans.

In addition, the core elements of a company's direction, purpose, vision, strategy, brand, and values are often not in alignment. The company's core reason for being, why it exists and therefore the purpose it serves in the world, is often not fully articulated or is captured just as a high-level statement. The brand may just be an aspirational perception of what the company once was or wishes to be, the strategy an analytically correct view of how the business should be able to perform based on arcane analyses and market moves. The result is that each provides some sense of direction for a transformation—but maybe all in different directions.

The best examples of companies that provide clear direction are those that create a well-integrated direction that puts purpose at the center of alignment between the vision, brand, strategy, and values. They are able to translate the directional concepts into clearly defined end-to-end experiences of customers, employees, and other stakeholders. These become descriptive stories that are easily communicated and understood. This makes the higher-level concepts come to life quite literally and puts a sense of passion into achieving the stated direction and delivering on the expectations and desires that customers, employees, and others have of the company based on its stated direction.

A One-Page View of the Future

When asked to create a short list of things learned from prior transformation experiences, the CEO of a $16 billion energy company noted that an often-overlooked element in successfully driving transformations is the "one-page" view of the entire direction. To illustrate the one-pager, he developed with his team a succinct summary of how the Purpose, Strategic Vision, Values, and Business Strategy all tied together in a cohesive and exciting direction. "It's memorable, easy to communicate, and easy to reference," he reflected. "If people can't remember the strategy, they can't act on it. And it is amazing how many times you need to communicate the same direction over and over again to get it to stick. So it has to be simple and memorable. The one-pager does that. And the hard work and real value comes up front in getting the executive team to make the tough decisions that allow you to focus the business so tightly that it can fit on one page." Figure 4.1 shows a generic form of a one-pager that has served many organizations well. We refer to it as the ACT Transformation Arrow.

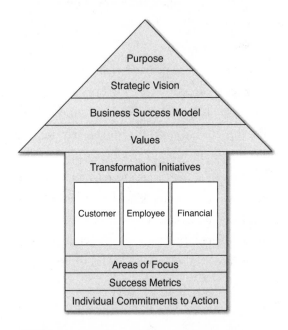

Figure 4.1 The ACT Transformation Arrow

The arrowhead consists of the four most fundamental elements required to set direction. The whys and whats of transformation are the Purpose of the enterprise, its Strategic Vision, the Business Success Model, and the Values that guide decision making and behaviors during execution. As a starting point, it is critical that these four elements are sharp and simple. This is the most important job the leadership team has following a thorough confrontation of reality.

The work that goes into developing a sharp point and getting the arrowhead pointed in the right direction starts with a broad look at the entire system. Then, like a ratchet, you take in the focus one crank at a time. Start with the internal and external views from the Confronting Reality Phase. Next, distill a Purpose and Strategic Vision. Then conduct a total system analysis of the company, comparing the current state versus the vision, to identify the biggest gaps using the template in Figure 4.2.[2]

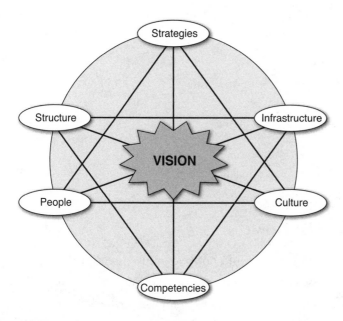

Figure 4.2 Total System Analysis Framework

Next, translate the largest gaps into a core set of Transformation Initiatives. The funnel in Figure 4.3 illustrates the process for narrowing down a Purpose and Strategic Vision to a focused set of corporate Transformation Initiatives. The remainder of this chapter covers practical ideas, templates, and exercises for developing your Purpose, Strategic Vision, and Business Success Model. The company Values and individual Commitments to Action, or CTAs, are also important parts of the arrow because they support and drive the corporate Transformation Initiatives. We will attend to them in the next chapter.

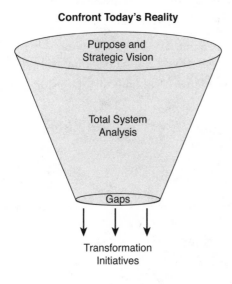

Figure 4.3 The Transformation Planning Funnel

Articulating a Purpose

A company's Purpose should not be confused with a concept of driving social causes or being mission-driven. Purpose in our strategic and transformation context relates to knowing why your company exists, what value it creates in the world, and how it contributes positively to others. For example, an iconic motorcycle company has a Purpose to "Fulfill dreams of personal freedom." A top performing

airline lives by the Purpose to "Connect people to what is most important in their lives." And an e-book platform company follows the Purpose "To make available in less than 60 seconds every book, ever
written, in any language...." What is common in the concept of Purpose and in these examples is that they are statements about bringing
value to others and are not defined by the assets or markets that the
company competes in today.

As a result, the Purpose is not confined to traditional market seg-
ment definitions and serves as an ambition for the organization to
continually strive to serve customers, employees, and partners better.
This leads to inspiration to drive teams to innovate, disrupt outdated
ways of competing, and draw out an emotional quality that puts people in the role of delivering value to others, not just going to work to
do a job. In fact, recent research indicates that over 90% of companies
either have or are developing a Purpose for their company. Further,
70% of leaders at these global companies believe it is important to
integrate Purpose into core business functions, with Purpose including a balanced view of value for customers, benefit for greater society, and financial returns for shareholders. However, the same report
indicates that only 37% say their business model and operations are
well aligned with their Purpose.[3]

Leveraged correctly, Purpose becomes a focal point and platform
to align the essence and definition of the company including the vision,
brand, values, and value proposition. It is also a powerful driver in
corporate transformations, which require high levels of engagement,
motivation, and passion at all levels to succeed. A clear Purpose also
provides a basis for setting investment priorities and making business
decisions. As an example, a retail pharmacy developed the Purpose of
"helping people on their path to better health" to motivate a transformation to a new type of blended retail and healthcare company. Using
the Purpose as a catalyst to reposition the company and reinvigorate
the organization, leaders realized that selling cigarettes in their stores
no longer fit with the Purpose of the company. In a bold move, the

company decided to stop selling cigarettes, which was approximately a $2 billion per year line of business. In the first quarter after making the bold move and sticking with their commitment to their Purpose, revenue increased by more than 10%.

Developing a Purpose for your company is not a trivial task. Although often communicated as an inspirational statement, Purpose is actually a much more complex concept that embodies the reason for being, the essence of what is different, the journey and path the organization is on, and what value it brings to the world. Begin with considering how the company started. What did its products or services do for customers that they weren't getting elsewhere? Think about why customers, employees, and other stakeholders are better off today because of what the company does and what attracts them in a magnetic way to the company beyond just the products and services. You can also look at the intersection of what is unique about the company's values, culture, brand, value proposition, and reputation and identify strong common threads. Within these various perspectives and explorations, you can develop your Purpose. A strong Purpose should be an active statement that focuses on the positive value you create for others, including customers, employees, as well as humanity in general. Purpose developed in this way becomes a north star to guide the strategic vision all the way through the entirety of the initiatives, operations, and culture shift in a corporate transformation.

Creating a Strategic Vision

Beyond Purpose, a clear view of what success may look like on the horizon is important as well. However, one of the most commonly heard strategic visions today is, "We want to be a market leader and to be an X billion-dollar player in our market." It's a statement about market position and financial gain. Those are fine aspirations, but a strategy to be an X billion-dollar player does not work well as a complete vision for focusing and aligning execution. Focusing on an end outcome metric without a clear articulation about the critical requirements to reach the goal allows the leadership team to demand results without providing direction. That does not produce the kind of focused alignment and execution needed to generate the break-through results the leaders are hoping to achieve. In addition, a vision that is only financially motivated leaves most people without any passion for achieving it, which is also a necessary component to achieving breakthroughs in performance and, hence, the need also for the articulation of a Purpose for the enterprise.

A Strategic Vision should serve as more than just an aspiration to achieve a numerical goal. Instead, the following are guidelines to use in judging the quality of your vision statement. A vision statement should

- State what employees will be doing or how markets will be responding when success is achieved.
- Clarify the general playing field (set boundary conditions).
- Specify which of the company's core competencies are unique.
- Signal an aspiration-driven level of achievement.

Some truly great Strategic Visions over time have never been achieved. Finite thinkers will say it's heresy to set a vision that isn't achievable. But visionaries know that a great vision continuously stretches execution by creating a constant tension between current success and greater possibilities. In contrast, finite visions have finite endings.

For example, Nordstrom's company vision has remained un-changed for more than 100 years since its establishment in 1901: "Offer the customer the best possible service, selection, quality, and value.[4] This clearly places service first, which is still the hallmark of Nordstrom's business. In another example, Microsoft's original vision was to see "A computer on every desk and in every home, running Microsoft software."[5] This sounded like a pipe dream at one point, but has been almost fully realized today. Just imagine if Microsoft stopped by saying, "We want to be a billion-dollar player and a market-leading operating systems company in the world." That would have been a very limiting vision compared to where the company's growth has taken it.

But where, exactly, should a transformation leader focus a company? Often it is useful to begin an executive session with a simple, but telling, exercise. Sometimes all it takes to get visioning started is a simple, projective exercise that involves members of the leadership team writing about what they believe their organization will have achieved or will look like in the future if the transformation they are planning is successful. Following a thorough Confronting Reality Phase, such a relatively quick and straightforward exercise usually enables the assembled decision makers to immediately identify the key strategic vision elements, which can then be refined to populate the very tip of the arrowhead and make it sharp. With such a simple intervention, the Purpose and Strategic Vision can be generated without having to waste months of committee work and elaborate brainstorming sessions that cause this second major step in the transformation planning process to bog down.

The process of developing a Purpose and Strategic Vision must be both creative and grounded in analysis. Projective techniques like the one discussed stimulate the creative process, which then needs to be grounded in an understanding of customers, competitors, and what employees are passionate about and capable of doing.

To be effective, they must be grounded in a rigorous Business Success Model, and, from that model, distilled into a few specific initiatives—each of which is tied to bold, but unambiguous outcome measures. Therefore, the next part of setting dear direction is to define the Business Success Model. Put plainly, this is how the company will allocate resources, keep score, and ultimately make money within the intent and scope of its unique Purpose and particular strategic vision.

Distilling the Business Success Model

The old Albert Einstein saying goes something like this, "The definition of insanity is continuing to do the same thing and expecting a different outcome." Similarly, in the work of leading transformations, you're not going to get very far along the path to a bold, new vision if you continue to allocate resources and measure progress the same ways you have done in the past. The essential vehicle for effectively reallocating your limited resources is to create a Business Success Model that is uniquely designed to test and support your new strategic vision. If developed at the company level, this success model should also reveal how you will grow the earnings stream so that you can increasingly improve your ability to access debt and equity sources to accelerate progress of your transformation. Finally, such a model should also reveal what businesses or activities need to be eliminated to free resources to support the momentum to the vision state.

In short, the Business Success Model is the engine that fuels the ability for the organization to reach the strategic vision and is the basis for both resource allocation and competitive differentiation.

Figure 4.4 shows a simple but very clear articulation of a Business Success Model. It reveals how the company will allocate resources differently, where it will invest for competitive advantage, and how that fits within the context of the overall corporate value chain. In this simple case, the Business Success Model supports a strategic vision for a company looking to differentiate based on staying ahead of competitors with technology and providing more value in customer service. More incremental funding will be devoted to technology (5%) and customer service (2%). To fund those differentiators, a focus on cost savings in the supply chain (–5%) and leveraging channel partners (–4%) will generate enough savings to net the company a 2% profitability advantage that can be used to go straight into earnings or to have additional pricing flexibility when needed compared with competitors. This simple articulation of the Business Success Model makes clear to all employees what their part of the organization specifically needs to contribute. In this case, the technology division's primary focus will be on innovation and speed to market. In strategic supply, the primary focus will be on cost savings. In the channels organization, creating large-scale partnerships will be critical; for customer service, the focus will be on high quality.

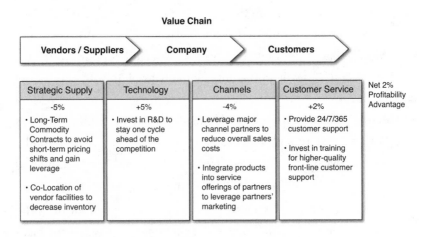

Figure 4.4 Business Success Model

Due Diligence on Yourself

A great example of what can be done to figure out the best Business Success Model quickly may be derived from the work of private equity investment firms. These firms buy companies using their own capital and debt, stay on as primary owners for several years while turning around or supercharging performance, and then sell the company at a gain. The cycle time up front for assessing the true value of a company and determining how much to pay for it is very short. This is known as the due diligence period. During that time, a very small team from the private equity firm will dig into the details of the target company's financials, operations, sales channels, customer service, and other supporting organizations to see where real value is generated and determine where there might be pockets that are underleveraged. They also look for high-risk areas.

This is the same information that corporations need to understand to develop their Business Success Model. It's the simple question of: "How does this business and industry really work, how does it create value, and what are the likely financial consequences of the model's success?" Often, the last step in business modeling is the development of a set of high-level pro forma financial statements that highlight the key success metrics. Sometimes in highly uncertain situations, the best you can do is lay out a set of alternative scenarios associated with performance consequences.

This up-front due diligence process has been referred to as similar to a physical exam, a *full* physical exam to be precise. It's not very enjoyable but is effective in telling you what is working and what is not. In a matter of days or weeks, the private equity firms are able to come up with an accurate picture of the target business and the underlying drivers of value.

How can they answer those tough questions so quickly? First, there is a short, relatively fixed time frame for them to make up their minds on a bid for a company. In the case of private equity, the deal will be lost to others if decisions can't be made quickly.

Corporate executives often underestimate the speed possible in quickly moving from planning to execution. Based on experience, it should only take a few weeks for a small group of people to develop an initial working vision and Business Success Model needed to launch the next phase of transformation in an organization.

Why do so many executive teams never reach the same level of depth and specificity of direction that private equity investors find in a matter of weeks? According to the managing principal in one of the large private equity firms with whom we have consulted,

There are a few common reasons we've found for management missing some of the drivers of value available to them. Often, people have not gone back and challenged cost allocations in the business, and the business has changed. As a result, they don't know where the real profitability is coming from. At times, people may have incentives to make a particular part of the business look better than it is. In addition, too much can be taken for granted in profit and cost expectations around the business based on high-level statements made by past executives and owners. People have a tendency to make things overly complex, and usually the real answers are pretty simple.

There is no reason that transformation leaders cannot conduct rapid due diligence on themselves, an essential front-end step in a successful corporate transformation process. The following are some tips for doing this yourself.

First, the analysis team needs to have a clear mandate and high-level support so that its members can raise and analyze all of the tough questions that others have been afraid to ask. One good way to cover all of the tough questions is to follow a due diligence checklist that is typically used in buyout situations to guide the work of the due diligence team. These lists include preset items that must be validated and include items such as the following:

Market

- Market size and growth of key business lines

Customers

- Customer loyalty and willingness to re-up contracts
- Value and quality of core products and technologies from external perspective
- Confirmation of differentiators from external sources

Competition

• Market share trends and competitive positioning

• Reasons for any recent competitive losses

Company

• Profitability by business unit

• Capabilities and loyalty of key employees

Leveraging this type of checklist ensures that the tough questions get addressed squarely and in the right depth, right up front. Not surprising, internal managers know where the skeletons are and will often try to protect certain data from seeing the light of day. In addition, due diligence teams often conduct customer as well as noncustomer interviews to serve as a vital reality check to balance against the internal-only views of people, processes, and technologies.

Finally, such due diligence teams will insist upon open access to and full candor with all members of the top executive team. In a transformation effort, often the internal due diligence team will consist of some operational vice presidents or directors with financial analysts in support. Then, after the Confronting Reality Session and fueled with the facts from the due diligence, the full executive team will engage in determining the biggest levers available for improving the Business Success Model. Based on the experience and knowledge within the executive team, members are broken into smaller teams to take on a prioritized set of issues associated with the Business Success Model for the purpose of fully assessing them and developing recommendations. Within a matter of three to four weeks, the senior team regroups to collectively wrestle with the various recommendations to improve the Business Success Model before they conclude on the highest-impact changes that need to be made. This prioritizing and focusing step is critical before moving on to make the more operational decisions.

Not surprising, it is essential for the leadership team to have an experienced objective third party to guide them safely and surely through their due diligence on themselves.

According to our private equity executive,

Private equity investors are often much more willing to push things to the edge to find the performance limits of a business than existing owners, which is another reason private investors can find new value in old companies. They typically are more willing to encourage management to take the risk of testing traditional limits.

Transformation Initiatives: The "Hows"

After you have refined your strategic vision and developed and tested the supporting Business Success Model, it is time to complete the focusing and alignment steps in your transformation launch process. You must carefully operationalize the *hows* of the transformation game plan: the Transformation Initiatives, or TIs.

This means making the tough decisions to net down the focus of the company's execution to a critical few, impactful, high-priority initiatives that everyone will be expected to execute with sustained rigor and courage. These major Transformation Initiatives are placed in the shaft of the Transformation Arrow.

From our direct involvement as principal process architect in dozens of successful CEO-led, enterprise-wide transformations, we have found that Transformation Initiatives operationalized in a certain manner have the best chance of success.

In a nutshell, here are the bare essentials...

In the shafts of the most successful Transformation Arrows that we have launched reside company-wide Transformation Initiatives, each of which is supported by a limited number of carefully selected

Areas of Focus and outcome metrics, all of which are tied to specific departmental Programs of Action and individual commitments to action for every soul in every component and at every level in the enterprise. There you have it. Now let's take a closer look.

Triage to Three Corporate Initiatives

An organization can pursue a maximum of three, possibly four, corporate-wide Transformation Initiatives to achieve quantum improvement in a short time period. Within those top-level initiatives, there needs to be a clear articulation of the areas of intense focus that, when tied to clear outcome metrics, will distinguish your particular transformation.

In fact, when it comes to the Areas of Focus within each initiative, we strongly recommend that they be strictly limited at the company or departmental level to just three, but not more than four for each initiative. If you start multiplying the number of initiatives times the number of Areas of Focus, you quickly realize that any more additions will overload the system. Then the components that you have so carefully crafted to accelerate execution will break down into incremental fragments that will Gridlock your people and resources.

This is a difficult discipline to follow for leaders. Picking just three initiatives and sticking with them takes some courage up front. As a leader or member of a leadership team, you need to provide clarity on the most high-impact ways for people to contribute to executing the strategy you are committed to achieving.

The CEO at one of our seasoned clients had dramatically turned around a global company and described the need for focusing this way: "In a large organization, we can say we have five things to do at the top. At the next level, each of those translates into ten tasks, and then ten more tasks on those ten, and so on. By the time it goes all the way down the organization, the time spent becomes enormous and spread out all over. You need to find just a few things that really matter, top to bottom, and focus on those."

Although every company is different, when given the challenge of focusing on three things, most companies typically end up with a similar set of nominal categories for Transformation Initiatives. One is typically focused on customers and specific customer needs. A second is focused on people and talent management. The third is typically focused on shareholders and financial performance. In some situations, companies have added a fourth initiative that is a critical problem for the business that needs a short-term focus, such as technology time-to-market, energy efficiency, digitalization, globalization, and so forth. We refer to this as the idiosyncratic initiative that finalizes the critical path toward the new Strategic Vision.

Although the core three are categorically very similar across successful transforming companies, each Transformation Initiative category becomes unique for each company in terms of the two to three Areas of Focus that are selected for each one of them to guide attention and allocate resources to drive them. For example, one company might focus on margins and pricing to drive their financial growth initiative, whereas another might select an acquisition strategy and new product development to achieve its financial growth initiative.

These few, major Transformation Initiatives become the critical link to translate between the market-oriented Strategic Vision and the operations-oriented tactical plans, which every person in the organization will carry as individual commitments. Every employee cannot participate directly in the setting of the Strategic Vision and Business Success Model. This is the responsibility of senior management. However, it is possible, indeed critical, for every employee to fully engage in how they will personally drive each of the key initiatives at their job level and within their sphere of influence.

The set of templates in Figure 4.5 illustrate a framework to operationalize the Transformation Initiatives at the company or department level. After this part of the shaft in the Transformation Arrow is clearly articulated, the next step is to achieve alignment among all the sub-units—that is, have them complete their versions of the templates and submit them for approval.

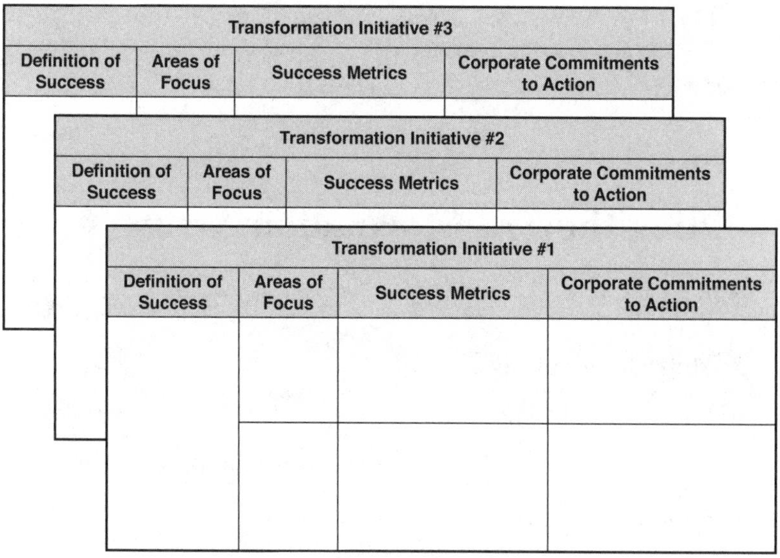

Figure 4.5 Transformation Initiative Templates

Next, you will need to use the *Rapid, High-engagement, All-employee Cascade* process to help managers and employees at all levels develop corresponding individual Commitments to Action, which will be covered in the next chapter, along with how to articulate corporate values that lead to needed behavior changes and to enable managers at all levels to help their employees set Commitments to Action that are aligned with the corporate Transformation Initiatives.

The result of these final components of the Transformation Arrow is the creation of a clear and compelling line-of-sight accountability from top to bottom in an organization for driving the Transformation Initiatives and living the company's Values.

Tips for Orchestrating the Focus Phase

- The antidote to organization Gridlock is focus. Focus your organization by setting clear direction and priorities starting at the top and through all levels.

- Do More ON Less. Focus everyone on just the critical few things that can contribute the most to turning your big ideas into big results.

Building the Transformation Arrow

Establish a Purpose and Strategic Vision for the organization that

- Motivates employees
- Focuses on the customer
- Clarifies the general playing field (sets boundary conditions)
- Specifies how the company is unique
- Signals an aspiration-driven level of achievement

Translate the Strategic Vision into a Business Success Model that

- Targets specific market and product areas
- Provides priorities to guide investment and funding decisions
- Indicates how profitability will be created across the company

Conduct due diligence on your own company (even when no transaction is pending) to quickly

- Identify untapped sources of growth and value
- Establish a true picture of profitability by unit or product line to drive decisions on focus and resource allocation
- Create a fact-based foundation for better business execution
- Actively test the limits of your business model

Shoot for three Transformation Initiatives, with no more than three Areas of Focus, each with specific Outcome Metrics

Endnotes

1. FranklinCovey, xQ Report Based on Harris Interactive Database. December 2003.

2. For more details on how to conduct a total systems analysis of your organization, refer to Robert H. Miles, "Leading Corporate Transformation: Are You Up to the Task?" in Jay A. Conger, Gretchen M. Spreitzer and Edward E. Lawler, III, *Leader's Change Handbook: An Essential Guide to Setting Direction and Taking Action.* San Francisco: Jossey Bass Publishers, Division of John Wiley & Sons, 1999, pp. 221–267.

3. EY Beacon Institute and Harvard Business Review Analytics, 2015.

4. Nordstrom, Inc., 2007, Nordstrom website at www.nordstrom.com.

5. Robert X. Cringely, "Getting Real How Microsoft Plans to Dominate Digital TV." *I, Cringely Weekly Column,* May 6, 1998. www.pbs.org/cringely/pulpit/1998/pulpit_19980507_000569.html.

5

The Align Phase

As your transformation Launch shifts to the Align Phase, you will need to continue the intensive work with your executive team to complete the remaining components of the Transformation Arrow and ensure that the top three levels of leaders, counting yourself, are fully committed before asking them to rapidly and consistently Cascade the commitment-setting process to all of their employees.

Left on your to-do list is the refinement and alignment of each Area of Focus and Success Metric by department for the corporate Transformation Initiatives. Then all members of the leadership team need to set their own Commitments to Action to support each Transformation Initiative. In addition, the transformation game plan is not complete until you identify the few important Values that support the Transformation Initiatives and to which Behavior Change Commitments must be made, starting with your leadership team.

Finally, once all members of the team have developed their aligned performance and behavioral change commitments, there is a need to pause for a serious *Stop Doing* exercise, as well as for your personal assessment of the earnestness of your team members before cascading the transformation to all managers and employees.

Let's take these critical elements of the Align Phase one at a time.

Absolute Alignment

As we have discussed, fragmented, under-resourced lists of ideas overlaid on an already overtaxed system are persistent nemeses along the path to transformation. This is what happens when you don't stick to a limited set of initiatives with full alignment at the top.

As the senior vice president of IT in one of our large retail company transformations has pointed out, "If you're not uncomfortable with how tight the initiatives are, they're not tight enough. The more tight and narrow the initiatives, the bigger impact they can have because people and resources will be leveraged to their best."

Individual Commitments to Action

The transition from transformation planning to doing involves setting individual *Commitments to Action (CTAs)*. The entire organization needs to engage in the process of developing and committing to act on a limited set of individual commitments that are in alignment with the Transformation Initiatives relevant to each employee's job scope.

The end goal of engaging the full organization in the process is to generate a situation in which all people are able to set specific Commitments to Action that are aligned to drive the overall results. These commitments need to be relevant for their level of contribution, aligned to support the top objectives, and things they were able to help design. The commitments need to be "their" promises to support the transformation. The odds of a person following through with excellence on commitments that they helped develop are much higher than just completing tasks assigned by others.

This step is often nonexistent in strategy communications sessions, which often take place as big kickoff events with lots of fanfare and little engagement or follow-through for results.

In performance management and goal-setting processes at many companies, the goals are set only between an employee and his or her direct manager, usually with no specific understanding about the company strategy and without any dialogue with the rest of the peer team on what is needed from that individual. The only documents discussed at an individual goal-setting session might be a copy of last year's performance review and a draft of the next year's performance review document for the individual. Such sessions usually devolve into a perfunctory administrative task of filling in blanks rather than having a real dialogue about priorities, personal commitments, and job design for the coming year.

In our work on a transformation at a global technology company, senior executives thought they had this aced. They believed that each employee at the company routinely set his or her individual business commitments at the beginning of each calendar year, to be reviewed semiannually as part of the performance management process. But when we examined the process in action, most individuals didn't get around to setting their commitments until June, just prior to the time of their semiannual performance appraisal!

The fix that we introduced with their transformation launch was to simultaneously hook the commitment setting and performance appraisal setting across the entire organization during the transformation cascade rollout. Using our *Rapid, High-engagement, All-employee Cascade* (discussed in detail in the next chapter), we were able to get individual commitments drafted, peer-reviewed, and approved in *one* high-engagement setting at each level in the businesses and functions. This enabled us to quickly achieve alignment from top to bottom in the organization and immediately ramp the cycle of transformation execution and learning for the full performance year. Many executives don't appreciate the need to do this—or are simply unaware that it is possible to do this—until they've missed their first-year Transformation Initiative targets by wide margins.

Alignment of Commitments Across "Silos"

Once the leadership team has worked through the steps to effectively confront reality, set the direction, and create Transformation Initiatives, many managers feel like the Commitment to Action part of the process is a break from the teamwork and a chance to take the team's plan and run to daylight with just their piece of the transformation. To some extent, they are correct. Personal commitments to action have to be set in every subunit and by every person in the organization. However, even with all the senior leaders having been intensively involved together in developing the transformation game plan, it is very easy for their commitments to get out of alignment across the business and functional groups.

With a simple exercise of writing each senior executive's commitments and those of their subunits on index cards and posting them on a wall, they all can see how their collective commitments mesh. So it is critical before rollout to vet the transformation game plan with the next level of leadership, which we call the Extended Leadership Team (ELT), whose members make up the leadership teams of each of the company's business units and functional departments. But more than that, members of the Senior Leadership Team should go through a quick round of exchanges with their peers of the commitments they have worked out with their own teams. Even though most of their perspectives will have been aired in earlier transformation dialogues with their peers, some interdependencies inevitably get overlooked, and gaps in coverage can surprise well into the transformation planning process. For this reason, a final planning meeting of the Senior Leadership Team that is dedicated to resolving dependencies and closing gaps is always a good idea. This brief pause doesn't have to be elaborate because the senior team has worked closely on all of the earlier launch steps.

This simple exercise at the end of the transformation planning process invariably surfaces obvious misalignments and unrecognized interdependencies, which can quickly be addressed. Often there are gaps in coverage that if not filled before rollout will retard performance during the Execution Phase. This extra step is well worth the taking.

To drive home the importance of alignment from top to bottom in an organization, consider the reflections of a CEO who was attempting to transform a perfectly good basic materials company into a great one. Looking back over the first year of his successful corporate transformation, he concluded that

> I think the business challenge that the ACT process handles beautifully is the congealing of the top leadership team on what you want done and then cascading it down so it is communicated to every employee.

His CFO, who had partnered with us on arranging the infrastructure to launch the transformation during that "good to great" challenge, chimed in similarly:

> A by-product of this process is that when you require a business leader—whether at the Senior Leadership Team or quarry manager level—to make presentations to their own people about their goals and commitments, they are really publicly stating what "we are going to accomplish." It makes those people realize they have to act as mentors or leaders. It's not just a selfish game anymore. These people to whom they've made the speeches are now watching to see if they are going to walk the talk.

Where Should Lightning Strike?

Another pitfall to avoid in setting Commitments to Action at the top is the tendency to assign sole functional responsibility for each Transformation Initiative. This traditional approach to goal setting may sometimes be sufficient during steady-state conditions. But when your company has to rise to a corporate transformation challenge, all hands, meaning all organizational components, are needed behind all of the major Transformation Initiatives.

In contrast, our experience is that management teams often mistakenly identify the "people" initiative as one that the Human Resources (HR) department should own and execute. However, if the VPs of all staff departments and business units do not sign up for individual commitments to improve the quality of people on their team, the people initiative targeted for quantum improvements in a short time period will be doomed to disappoint.

Successful people strategies cannot be owned only by HR— they need to have full commitment and active involvement from the Senior Leadership Team, which represents all components of the organization; every leader on that team should have a reasonable set of personal commitments to action to support that type of initiative. A general manager can make a commitment to deliver the key programs HR will develop, such as 360° reviews, improved recruiting and interviewing processes, or succession planning. This way, when a manager's team is asked to get involved in the initiatives, it is to support their boss and their team's goals, not just to respond to being told to do something by another department. This holds true for all other types of initiatives as well. Responsibility for growth, quality, or product development, as further examples, must be squarely borne by all members of the leadership team and the parts of the organization for which they are responsible, not just by the department that specializes in a particular initiative.

As a general rule, then, *all* members of the Senior Leadership Team should be responsible, albeit with varying weights, for *all* of the Transformation Initiatives. Each should be able to get behind at least some of each initiative's Areas of Focus and Action Programs. And all of the levels and components of the organization can have an impact on the growth and people initiatives, as examples; not just the Sales and HR departments, respectively. Indeed, even the lowest-level job holder in an enterprise can find legitimate and useful ways to formulate personal commitments to drive these and other Transformation Initiatives. So don't fall into the "this is my turf" trap. When corporate transformation is the challenge, you'll need all the help you can get from other parts of the enterprise.

Working on the alignment of the initiatives up front and across the organization will ensure that team members in different work groups will all be working under priorities and tactics that are mutually reinforcing. Silo conflicts are reduced, and greater execution results.

Alignment of Values

One indispensable element in generating and keeping alignment is the living of shared company Values. Every day, people in the organization will be faced with making decisions that will either move the organization forward or not. Living by a core set of Values allows individuals to make decisions on situations that haven't been addressed before and to stay in alignment with the transformation as they make those decisions, when you and others aren't around to help them think through things. Values should be tied to specific, desired behavior changes as part of the transformation.

Bedrock values—the ones you might find in the Boy Scout Code—begin to be developed in employees, not when they arrive in a company, but when they start out their lives. They are the result of the confluence of parental supervision, role modeling by respected peers and adults, and trial and effort in the real world. These are the kinds of things we hope and definitely ought to screen for when we select people for employment in our company. Without such traits, which are part and parcel of being a good person and a good citizen, no organization can sustain itself, much less flourish.

However, an additional Values dimension is needed in companies, particularly those attempting a corporate transformation. In this dimension are the company values selected by the leadership team, which are aligned with and that uniquely support your Transformation Initiatives. Such Values are needed to guide the behavior changes required at all levels to ensure transformation success. Our experience has consistently revealed that the best results on this dimension are achieved when the chosen company Values are tied directly to the three to four Transformation Initiatives.

To illustrate, during the turnaround of a global "big box" retailer following a disallowed merger with a rival, the new CEO and executive team eventually selected three primary initiatives to launch the revitalization of their company. They said to all constituencies that they wanted the company to become the "most compelling place in the industry to Invest, Shop, and Work." Underlying these catchy categories, they developed a limited set of Areas of Focus and Metrics to focus and drive their turnaround:

- *Invest*—Shareholder value creation
- *Shop*—*Customer* satisfaction
- *Work*—Employee retention and reengagement

When they turned to select the Values that made the most sense to emphasize during the transformation effort, they had a long list that had been posted in all the conference rooms by the previous regime. After some structured dialogue, the team relatively quickly decided that an emphasis on three particular Values made the most sense and could probably make the greatest contribution during the first year, given the selected initiatives. The Values they singled out for special attention were

1. *Respect for the individual*—The company's employee base was quite diverse, so this value was believed to be a critical factor in achieving the Best Place to Work initiative.

2. *Fanatical customer service*—During the long wait for approval of its acquisition by a rival retailer, which was ultimately denied by the Department of Justice, the company had lost its focus on

the customer. Driving value in customer service was viewed as critical to creating the best place to shop.

3. *Excellence in execution*—During all the turmoil, the company and its employees had also lost their focus on execution. This value was designed to help encourage the restoration of excellence in execution, which, in turn, would contribute to their becoming the best place to invest in their industry category.

Figure 5.1 shows how the Transformation Initiatives, Outcome Metrics, and Values were clearly aligned, making the business drivers and values mutually reinforcing. This alignment greatly simplifies and focuses both operational and personnel or cultural efforts on the same initiatives. It is easier for people at all levels to understand, remember, and execute.

Values	Respect for the Individual	Fanatical Customer Service	Excellence in Execution
	↕	↕	↕
	The Most Compelling Place to…		
Transformation Initiatives	Work	Shop	Invest
Area of Focus	Employee Retention and Engagement	Customer Satisfaction	Shareholder Value Creation
First-Year Outcomes	72% Improvement in Employee Retention	50% Reduction in Customer Complaints	From "Worst 10" to "#2" among S&P 500 on Shareholder Value Creation

Figure 5.1 The Performance-Values Nexus

Success was far from guaranteed, however. They had 900 stores, and they needed realignment and engagement at all those stores very quickly, and they needed to do it in a terrible recessionary year. By the end of the first year of execution, the retailer achieved the following breakthrough results on its Transformation Initiatives:

1. *Invest*—The company moved from the "Worst Ten" in shareholder value creation to Number 2 among S&P 500 firms.

2. *Shop*—50% reduction in customer complaints.

3. *Work*—72% increase in employee retention.

The CEO later reflected that it was, "a proven methodology that says if you apply these tools, you can accelerate the engagement of the whole entire organization."[1]

The Values-Performance Nexus

After the core Values are identified, they need to be anchored in individual commitments to behavior changes, initially at the top, starting with the CEO and his or her direct reports and then throughout the entire enterprise.

When Transformation Initiatives are brought together with aligned company Values in the performance management system of a transforming enterprise, the stage is set (as shown in Figure 5.2) for rapid achievement of breakthrough results in terms of both business outcomes and culture change.[2]

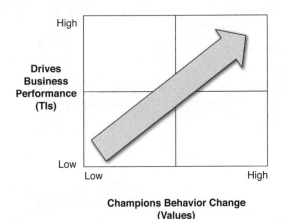

Figure 5.2 Rapid Transformation Success

Structuring Widespread Commitment

To support an accelerated corporate transformation, individual CTAs must be made by everyone in the organization—yes, everyone from the CEO to the last person in the door. And this must be accomplished simply, smoothly, and rapidly once the leadership team has completed the Transformation Arrow. How to accomplish this rapidly—actually *in a single sitting* at each organizational level—will be described in detail in the next chapter. Here it is important to demystify the apparatus that we have successfully used over and over to structure everyone's CTAs.

Believe it or not, we use the same structured format to capture and record the CEO's commitments as we deploy to first-line employees. It couldn't be simpler.

Recall that we not only want to set performance commitments to drive the Transformation Initiatives, but also Behavior Change Commitments to live the Values that support the Purpose and Strategic Vision. To capture the CTAs of every person in the enterprise, we use the templates shown in Figure 5.3. We start by completing the CEO's CTAs and then systematically but quickly work all the way down through the organization. Each individual first completes one version of the top form for each Transformation Initiative before completing the form at the bottom for his or her Behavior Change Commitments.

When filling out the CTA forms, we have found it useful to offer a simple set of guidelines—an old but always reliable checklist. We ask everyone to make their commitments S-M-A-R-T.

S: SPECIFIC

Is the CTA clear, understandable, and well defined?

M: MEASURABLE

Can the results of the CTA be quantified?

A: ALIGNED

Does the CTA fit with higher-level and adjacent CTAs?

R: RELEVANT

Is the CTA the best way that I can contribute to the achievement of higher-level CTAs, and do I have the authority, knowledge, and skill to fulfill the CTA?

T: TIME-BASED

Have I given the CTA a completion date?

Performance Commitments to Action
Performance Appraisal – Example

Team Member Performance Appraisal		
Name: Title:	Division: Location:	
Supervisor:	Title:	
Assessment: Year:	Q1 ☐ Q2 ☐ Q3 ☐ Annual ☐	

Corporate Initiative	Title:	Areas of Focus
Profitable Growth	1	Drive Margin
	2	Drive Growth

Area of Focus	Commitments to Action	Metrics	Time Frame	Comments	Rating*

* S=Superior, ER=Exceeded Requirements, MR=Meets Requirements, N=Needs Improvement, U= Unsatisfactory

Behavioral Change Commitments
Performance Appraisal – Example (Continued)

	Team Member Performance Appraisal		

Value	Behavioral Change Commitment	Comments	Rating*
Respect			
Play to Win			
Customer First			

Supervisor's Comments:

Supervisor's Rating [   ]

Reviewed with Team Member

Team Member:	Date:
Supervisor:	Date:

Team Member Comments:

Figure 5.3 Individual Commitments to Action

The First "Stop Doing" Pause

So far, you've used structured dialogue in a compressed format of launch meetings to confront reality and to develop Purpose, Strategic Vision, and Business Success Model components of the Transformation Arrow that are motivating, focusing, and challenging. You've worked closely with your team to articulate only a few major Transformation Initiatives, each with a limited set of Areas of Focus to drive attention, resource allocation, and execution. You've also feathered in agreement on a few company Values and used them to obtain behavior change, in addition to performance commitments from your leaders. The last step before aligning your organization with a major transformation launch or strategy execution effort involves deciding what *not* to do. This is the step many transformation leaders skip over only to pay for dearly later in the Execution Phase. Making the tough trade-offs about what to stop so that resources can be allocated to the most important initiatives is not easy. But it is essential to moving the organization into a Doing More ON Less mode for transformation success.

Think of your first "Stop Doing" exercise with your leadership team as an essential whistle stop on the tracks leading to full Cascade and full Execution. It is a major transformation step, but it can be so simple. Just assemble your leadership team. Give them advance notice that unless this step is successful, they'll end up having to do more with less in leading their parts of the corporate transformation. And ask them to prepare by working with their department team on identifying and prioritizing activities that do not lie on the critical path of the transformation game plan.

Instruct them that anything is fair game but that most progress in their triage effort will come from focusing on projects and programs in their own subunits over which they have direct control. Tell them not to forget standing committees and meetings, procedures and approvals, and reports.

Make sure that when you convene the SLT, whose members presumably have run all of this for full discussion with their own leadership team, you properly set up the Stop Doing meeting by reminding everyone about the *safe passage* rules, the *structured dialogue* guidelines, and the *tablework* procedures. That will help you keep emotions in check as your executives struggle with identifying give-ups that they otherwise would prefer to protect.

From the tablework with your SLT, capture all of the nominated candidates and then distill the candidates for elimination into the following categories: meetings, reports, processes/approvals, and projects. Write each candidate for elimination on a Post-It.

Then, within each category, rate each candidate for elimination on two criteria:

1. Complexity—(1) The idea is within my own personal control to stop doing; (2) the idea requires my own group or department to stop doing; or (3) the idea requires people, groups, or departments outside my own area to stop doing.

2. Impact—(1–3) The lower the number, the smaller the amount of time or money being saved by a Stop Doing decision. The higher the number, the larger the amount of time or money saved.

Make the ratings transparent to all by posting them on a matrix like the one in Figure 5.4 for each category. It should be easy to distill from this display the candidates that are the most complex and impactful.

Focus the assembled group of senior executives on the candidates for elimination that have close to or equal to 3 on either rating. Candidates having lower ratings should be referred back to the sponsoring subunit for resolution.[3]

Without this kind of structure and process, getting the key leaders of your transformation to put their pet projects and sacred cows on the chopping block could be quite challenging.

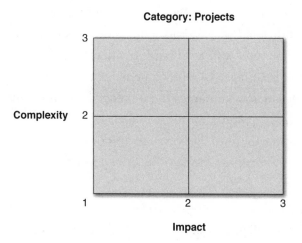

Figure 5.4 "Stop Doing" Matrix

And be forewarned: Essential as it is to have a rigorous "Stop Doing" exercise before shifting into the Cascade and Execution Phases, it will not be the only time you will need to do this exercise. People are timid at first to give up things to which they are personally committed. And early in a transformation process, many are not convinced that the transformation leader will stay the course. So you may have to conduct repeats during the first year of execution and certainly one before you replan and relaunch your second year of transformation. In general, the more you hold people accountable for results on the key Transformation Initiatives, the more interested everyone will become and the more proactive they will be in removing projects from their agendas that don't fall on the transformation critical path.

Put Your Money Where Your Game Plan Is

We often define transformation as "A few well-articulated initiatives targeted for breakthrough performance in a short period of time ... in a sea of necessary incremental improvements."[4]

With this perspective on the essence of corporate transformation in mind, this shouldn't have to be said, but unfortunately it needs to be said: When the three to four Transformation Initiatives have been agreed upon, there must be a fundamental realignment of the budget and a reallocation of resources that reflects their importance in the scheme of the corporate transformation challenge. These new initiatives must impact the way that investment decisions are made and cause a realignment of budgets to reflect the new priorities they represent.

Too often, the transformation game plan and new strategy and business model are not aligned with operating budgets. In some companies, the strategic planning process is done by the CEO and the Senior Leadership Team, budgeting is run separately by Finance, and performance goals and management are programs run by Human Resources. In addition, it is insufficient to create an "incremental" budget for the corporate Transformation Initiatives, in which only a small percentage of the total operating budget is set aside to fund these key initiatives. Such underfunding will surely result in an increased overlay of initiatives that add to Gridlock and fail to properly incentivize alignment and commitment to the new Transformation Initiatives. Nothing less than a full alignment of the Purpose, Strategic Vision, Business Success Model, Values, Transformation Initiatives, and individual Commitments to Action with Budgets will provide the organization-wide focus and sustained energy to break the pattern of continuing to add to task overload and organizational Gridlock.

The Bottom Line on Alignment

If your objective is to generate strategic alignment quickly, which is what is required to transform a company or a major component of it, you need absolute alignment starting at the top. If you have any misalignment at the top, it will only become magnified as it goes down through the organization. Big leaders cast large shadows! And if you encourage one department to try to "change the world" while permitting another to focus on the "same old, same old," you will be setting up both departments—as well as the corporate transformation you hope to achieve—for failure. So be careful about considering plans that get parts of the organization out of sync or even working at odds with each other.

There are several games the "laggards" in a transformation may play when attempting to drive the transformation into full execution. For instance, even relatively skeptical team members might be willing to participate in the early stages involving the development of a new Purpose, Strategic Vision, and Business Success Model. Given a strong commitment by the leader, these savvy managers will understand that they cannot avoid participating in the development of the new direction. But although they may play well on the front end of this creative process, they often avoid putting all their cards on the table. Instead, they play a game of poker—watching others turn over their cards to ensure they can win in the end when resource allocation decisions and commitments to organization changes are made. These increment lists typically come up with many "small adjustment" ideas in hopes that the transformation process won't really impact what they do on a daily basis.

One of the most common ways to avoid full commitment to corporate transformation and strategy execution is to argue for a continuation of "baseline funding" while making new incremental investments on the strategic initiatives. Incrementalists often argue that because a majority of revenue is derived from the current business, disruption needs to be minimized. Unfortunately, the perpetuation of these tactics in the face of major transformational challenges ensures the continued pursuit of the status quo.

The critical few Transformation Initiatives, by contrast, are targeted for quantum improvements in a relatively short period of time. The initiatives are not intended to be new incremental projects. By both definition and the way they are created, if they don't cause priorities up and down the full organization to shift, dramatic performance improvement won't unfold through the whole system.

Another common "head-fake" is introducing the idea of a pilot test. This is not to be confused with the useful practice of launching innovative start-ups within larger companies. In those cases, a skunk works approach can be quite valuable. However, when a full transformation of the core business is being launched, a toe-in-the-water approach won't get you across the English Channel, even on a calm day.

The argument goes something like this. "These strategic ideas sound like real breakthroughs in thinking. Very different from what we do today. To make sure we get it right, why don't we set up a pilot in a closed environment where it won't impact customers in any way? We'll see how things go there and really perfect the model in a safe environment. Then after we've got that done, we can roll it out and bring it to customers." Again, this sounds supportive and logical. However, internal "lab" pilots also allow the majority of the organization to sit tight and avoid change for a considerable period of time, time that can be valuable to competitors and very frustrating to customers and suppliers. Moreover, such pilots often founder for lack of support from the complete executive team. Even if they eventually work, critical time has been lost, and often they are tagged as being limited to only theoretical applications, and the incrementalists will find other reasons to avoid the transformation. And critical timing is often at the core of successful responses to ever-compressing cycle times and relentless threats from disruptive competitors.

The launches of successful corporate transformations have to unfold rapidly and start having customer impact early. You must get to Execution as soon as possible. You'll be moving into new territory, and you need to quickly get the cycle of learning from doing up and running. You'll not succeed if you become convinced by others to delay Execution until the 100% solution is firmly in hand.

Gut Check on Commitment

As the leader of corporate transformation and strategy execution, you have to challenge the full organization to align with the major strategic shifts that the team has committed to achieve. This starts at the very top. Active resisters from the onset of transformation planning must be confronted and, if necessary, removed from their posts. But for executive leaders on your team perched on the fence—somewhere between tentatively withholding support from or passively championing the new order—give them an opportunity to participate in designing the transformation game plan, working within the proven process architecture that we have been discussing. Allow them to provide input, share their ideas, shape the initiatives, and plan the rollout. But before moving into the employee Engage Phase, circle back with each one of them to determine if they are solidly on board. As one of our seasoned transformation CEOs cautions, "Remove 'change resisters' and people who 'pretend' to go along with the transformation but foot-drag or back-stab."

Tips for Simplifying the Align Phase

- **Achieve *absolute alignment* from top to bottom:**
  - Quickly address even small deviations from the focus at the top as these get magnified going down—senior executives cast big shadows.
  - Drive accountability throughout the entire organization through setting aligned and relevant individual Commitments to Action at all levels.
  - Restack all priorities top to bottom or you will, by definition, only be playing on the margins with incremental changes. This will make many people uncomfortable, but it is necessary.

- Reset investment and operating budget levels to align with the corporate Transformation Initiative prioritized Areas of Focus.
- Establish clear guidelines for resource allocation that will enable you to quickly identify and eliminate projects that are not on the transformation critical path.

- **Align values and behaviors:**
  - Select a few Values for focus that strategically align with the corporate Transformation Initiatives.
  - Anchor the Values in individuals' Behavior Change Commitments at all levels in the organization, starting with the CEO.
  - Pause for a "Stop Doing" exercise to align priorities and resource allocation. Plan to do this more than once during the first year of the corporate transformation.
  - Quickly address and handle any situations where leaders will not align fully.

Endnotes

1. For a more complete treatment of Values, refer to an earlier work of Robert H. Miles: *Leading Corporate Transformation: Blueprint for Business Renewal,* San Francisco: Jossey-Bass Publishers, a Division of John Wiley & Sons, 1997, especially pp. 51–53.

2. Brian O'Connor, "Anatomy of a Turnaround," *FastTrack Magazine*, Summer 2002, pp. 42–47.

3. We wish to acknowledge the contribution of our colleague, William Kemp, a Founding Partner at Enovation Partners, in helping to refine the "Stop Doing" exercise. He served as the internal ACT Process Architect on one of our recent CEO-led corporate transformations.

4. Robert H. Miles, "Accelerated Corporate Transformation (ACT): An Overview," Corporate Transformation Resources, 2013, p. 3.

6

The Engage Phase

Rapidly Engaging the Full Organization

How can you engage and energize thousands of employees within a matter of weeks?[1]

Leaders don't generally raise that question because they are not aware that such a feat can be accomplished in a rapid, reliable manner. But it's one of the major questions they should be asking when challenged with taking charge and launching the next major phase in an organization. In fact, many transformation efforts stall at this specific point because the great ideas and strategies at the top never make it far enough down in the company to have a true impact on employees and customers—which is where it really matters.

Past efforts, they recall, can take months—if not years—to roll out from top to bottom. More often than not, these efforts were implemented as one-off programs, not integrated into normal business operations, and conducted by consultants or specialized staff facilitators. Those other types of programs end up as overlays to the business and don't leverage the natural chain of command. They ultimately get replaced or just run out of energy before they generate any big results.

No wonder a recent study of American workers revealed that only one in ten employees has a clear line of sight between their job tasks and their company's goals. Moreover, only half of the surveyed employees felt that there was any follow-through with discipline from above on key priorities.[2]

The problem with these approaches is that by the time the message reaches the full organization, the top has already moved to new challenges and launched new strategies, putting the system out of alignment. And as you'll see, a message delivered by anyone other than the direct manager will not drive Execution down to the next level.

It's All About Engagement

The largest immediate boost in performance that companies get following the transformation process that we have outlined is a dramatic increase in employee engagement, which translates to immediate leaps in results across all dimensions of the business. Sometimes, the improvements start to build even before new initiatives have been fully implemented from the top. Does that surprise you? It's surprising to many leaders. Creating a fully engaged workforce, one where individuals bring their best every day, is a necessary element to generating great results. An engaged workforce is one in which people have passion for their roles and continually look for ways to contribute to their organization's performance.

We clearly all hope to be able to attract people like this. Indeed, if we do only a halfway decent job of hiring, our organizations should be filled with high-energy, creative-thinking people, who make up high-performance teams that are driving big results. But many of those bright eyes soon turn dim with experience in a given organization. Many of the great employees we hire soon begin to feel underutilized, marginalized, and disengaged all too soon. Indeed, a study of 840,000 employees of multinational companies revealed that employee satisfaction begins dropping at six months, and then it bottoms out at about three to five years.[3] Those in leadership positions are clearly not engaging their teams effectively.

Quantum Leaps

For several years, a large, public utility company facing impending deregulation struggled to generate a more competitive and high-performing workforce. The chart in Figure 6.1 clearly shows that during the three years prior to the ACT-based intervention, very little overall movement occurred on various dimensions of employee satisfaction and engagement. The year immediately following the Launch of a high-engagement, ACT-based transformation, quantum improvements were achieved across all dimensions of measured employee satisfaction and engagement throughout the 92 unionized plants in the company's portfolio.[4] Such a shift in attitude resulted in $400 million in cost savings, a major reduction in grievances, and huge improvements in safety.

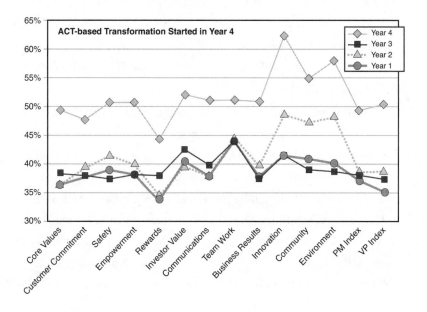

Figure 6.1 ACT-based Employment Engagement Leap

Source: Robert H. Miles, *Leading Corporate Transformation: Blueprint for Business Renewal.* New York: Jossey-Bass Publishers, a Division of John Wiley & Sons, 1974, p. 123.

This is a clear picture of what can happen when attitudes shift based on high engagement. The leap in performance was driven by a shift in engagement. Union employees just needed to be engaged in thinking through how to operate their area of responsibility differently under the company's new transformation agenda, not be told what to do and how to do it.

"Back in Black" Friday

What does a quantum leap in employee engagement look like, and what does it do for you in leading a transformation effort? At a national retail company, sales had been on a constant downward slide for five years. In fact, the company believed that perhaps its brand had been totally forgotten and it might need to change its name. There were also big challenges coming from new competitors and business model shifts that needed to be made. It was about halfway through the performance year when the new CEO and COO decided to apply the ACT process to accelerate a transformation they had called for at the beginning of the year.

For retailers, Black Friday refers to the Friday after Thanksgiving, the day that many retailers finally go beyond break-even profitability and go from being in the "red" (losing money) to being in the "black" (making money). It is typically the single day of the year that has the highest sales. It is a huge indicator for retailers each year on how they are performing overall. After engaging the full organization from the top executives through to the cashiers and warehouse staffs in early August, the company experienced a large jump in employee engagement, taking them from the competitive bottom quartile to the top half compared to similar companies.

That leap in engagement felt good to the executives, but would it translate into results? By the time Black Friday results were being tallied, they knew the answer was yes. With no major increase in mass advertising spending, the company had generated the largest sales day in the entire company history (including the heydays that had long since passed). It put them on track to have the first profitable full year and full year of positive year-over-year growth in same-store sales in the recent past. What had changed? The marketing and merchandising teams had been engaged by the new executives for weekly creative thinking sessions, store employees were allowed to prioritize serving customers over taking inventory, and everyone felt as though they had some say in how to do their jobs better every day. At that point, there had been no rebranding and no massive ad spending to bring customers back—there had just been a simple reengagement and focusing of the entire team.

Following the close of the year, the executive team was discussing the great results, and one executive asked what the team thought was the key: "What have we actually implemented or done differently?" One of the operations staff managers put it best this way, "Maybe that's what happens when you get 14,000 people engaged and excited again."

Employee Engagement Is Not Barbeque

But not all engagement attempts bear such bountiful fruit. One ill-fated attempt to increase rank-and-file employee engagement involved a planned "evangelical" event. It was conducted by an iconic high-tech company in Silicon Valley during the height of the 1990s boom. The company had well-branded products, but more standard alternatives had virtually devoured its business. Barely clinging to a 3% domestic market share, executives at the company decided to make a major push to reengage their workforce.

Plans were carefully laid to transport all employees to a local fairground where company leaders would hold forth with a big-screen, multimedia appeal to all hands, which outlined the new vision for the company, sketched the broad outlines of some new initiatives, and called for a return to the values and behaviors that had once made the company great. Ranging somewhere between a religious tent revival and a Big Ten pep rally, the event amounted to a great exhortation by executive leaders for all employees to perform differently and better on the job, all reinforced by lots of pyrotechnics and scheduled applause.

A week later, a key team member who attended the event said that all he could recall with clarity was the quality of the barbeque!

Clearly, this is not the pathway to employee understanding, commitment, and engagement. But generating engagement is essential to achieving breakthrough results.

Observing failed attempts like this one led to the design of a comprehensive but streamlined vehicle for rapidly creating "leaders at all levels" in a transforming enterprise. Our approach to employee rollout of a transformation game plan is simple, streamlined, and fast—an intervention that combines the benefits of employee training and communication with engagement, alignment, and performance management *in one sitting*.

The following section highlights some general design elements of this proven process architecture, which enables leaders to create rapid and effective engagement, which then leads directly to formal commitment and accountability. Some of the elements we explore with you may sound trivial. But success with employee engagement comes from the cumulative impact of a few very monumentally magnificent trivial choices.[5]

Spreading High Engagement

Imagine that an executive team has been working collaboratively to confront reality, create a strategy, and determine focus for the organization. How do you get the rest of the organization engaged? Surprisingly, it is the same method for how the top team became engaged. They experienced and made sense of the transformation game plan during their Cascade meetings in which was embedded a similar round of tablework modules, all based on the same principles of "safe passage" and "structured dialogue," much the same as the Senior Leadership Team had used to create the transformation game plan. It's this simple:

- Structure the Cascade encounter around the elements in the Transformation Arrow. Devote a module to each element in the Arrow.

- Choose for each module at each supervisor-led table a Facilitator, Recorder, and Presenter for the tablework exercise.

- Pause after the opening presentation in each module for the immediate supervisors to explain its relevance to their team before sharing the Commitments to Action (CTAs) they had made in the previous Cascade session one level above.

- Allow a few precious moments for personal reflection. Silence! (What does this Transformation Initiative, for example, mean for me? For us? How can we support our supervisor's commitments?)

- Open the session for structured dialogue and feedback.

- Challenge and expect individuals to translate the plans into personal CTAs. ("What does it mean for me?")

- Instruct each team member to record his or her preliminary personal CTAs before sharing them with his or her supervisor and team members.

- Briefly allow team members to refine and record their preliminary CTAs based on what they learned from the sharing exercise.

- Finalize these CTAs in a meeting between the supervisor and the team member within five days so that the member can swiftly set the next level Cascade session in which the process is repeated with his or her direct reports. (This rapid, high-engagement, double-looped cascade process is how we create top-to-bottom-aligned commitments and do so in a leader-led manner.)

We will provide specific illustrations of these modules later in the chapter.

Critical Importance of Dialogue

As we discussed before, dialogue is a critical element of successful engagement and commitment. Yet there is a natural tendency among executives and staffers when pressed for time to cut dialogue out of important meetings and other forums. Perhaps these executives think that if they just concentrate enough on communicating clearly, employees will "get it" and get on with it. Nothing could be further from the truth. As we've said, we use the same form of structured dialogue to bring employees aboard during well-defined Cascade meetings as we have described earlier with the work of the Senior Leadership Team and Extended Leadership Team during the Launch Phase to craft and refine the corporate transformation game plan and to bring their subunit leadership teams aboard. Even the senior-most executives don't get it until they become engaged in the ACT-based manner.

Hear It from My Boss

There is an old saying that employees join companies but leave bosses. Employees at each level experience "reality" at work as the one that their direct supervisor creates. To accentuate this point, a recent employee survey at a global company asked employees how they would like to receive important corporate communications. By a huge margin, they preferred direct verbal communication with their direct manager. And when it comes to hearing about and adjusting to new strategic directions or initiatives announced from above, the question employees really want answered, and answered from their boss who evaluates their performance, is "How important is this, and how will it impact our daily work—and me specifically?"

This general approach to engaging everyone in the organization is predicated on the belief that there is tremendous power each of us has to dramatically impact an entire organization, no matter what our standing or rank.

Joe Montana, Hall of Fame quarterback of the San Francisco 49ers, stressed the importance of this idea in a story he told us about a rookie player who had just joined his team.[6] "The first day of practice I threw him passes, and he kept dropping them. It was kind of embarrassing as the ball bounced off him and slipped through his hands." Not the kind of performance you would expect in this highly competitive situation. Then Joe continued, "But finally, he caught his first pass. Normally, in practice a receiver would run about ten yards after catching a pass, jog back, throw the ball in, and wait in line to do the drill again. Not this kid. The rookie tucked the ball away, turned up field, and sprinted full-speed to the goal line sixty yards away." And he kept sprinting for touchdowns every time he caught the ball in practice, even as veteran players ribbed him about having to wait and joked about what he was doing." The rookie Joe was describing was Jerry Rice, currently the only player to score over 200 touchdowns in a career in the National Football League.

Jerry's odd rookie behavior became a challenge to other veteran receivers on the team to step up and to the defensive players to try to stop him in practice. As Joe described it, the rookie changed the way the whole team practiced and played. The impact of one person willing to step out from the crowd and risk going beyond "normal" behavior is how entire cultures get changed. It takes a willingness to challenge the rest of your team to rise to a new level of excellence— even those veterans or people with higher standing. In too many cases, managers at all levels are kept in place as followers by self-imposed limits. They merely allow or enable changes to occur by simply follow-ing what they are told.

In the *Rapid, High-engagement, All-employee Cascade* process we are about to describe, these same managers are called into action to actively lead execution of the Transformation Initiatives in their part of the organization, no matter what level or standing they have. And to do this right, each person in a leadership position needs to be willing to create a setting in which even rookie receivers who may ini-tially drop the ball can have a big impact. Such leaders need to do this by first stepping up and out on to the limb to set bold commitments to support the major Transformation Initiatives, as well as commitments to visible behavior changes to live the values.

Then they need to set up their own rapid, high-engagement Cascade event using the principles and templates we have been dis-cussing to make it safe for their direct reports to take risks to change the status quo and set new and different commitments to drive the transformation game in their level and sphere of influence. This is a tall order, so you have to get the Engage Phase right. That's how you'll achieve quantum improvements across the enterprise in a short period of time.

Enough about broad concepts on how to proceed with a Rapid, High-engagement, All-employee Cascade to drive your transforma-tion game plan. Let's now focus on how to actually conduct one and use it as a model for participants to do the same for their direct reports down the line.

The Rapid, High-Engagement, All-Employee Cascade

Executives, particularly those launching and leading corporate transformations, must learn how to simply focus the organization in such a way that employees can quickly align. They must find new ways to engage employees so that they can lead the organization in new directions at all levels. Moreover, the increasing speed of change in general is forcing the need to engage and align all employees rapidly.

Such trends cause us to bolt an employee supercharger on to the traditionally management-focused process for leading a corporate transformation. The supercharger is the *Rapid, High-engagement, All-employee Cascade*. We know, a mouthful! But every element of the term is critical to its success.

This unique kind of Cascade must roll out in the organization *rapidly* because employees live in a dynamic world full of distractions. Often they are skeptical that senior management will hold the course, so movement quickly to early results helps keep energy and commitment high. Moreover, it greatly undermines unified effort if important parts of the organization have to wait too long after others have already gone through the transformation engagement process. Indeed, one of us once worked on a corporate transformation in which a three-person team of HR training professionals was sent out to deliver a four-day Cascade program, loaded with lots of employee training and HR policy modules in addition to the elements of the transformation game plan and associated commitment setting activities, to 100,000 employees around the world. When they returned two years later, their work had been lapped by another wave of new strategies!

There are many other reasons why the Cascade rollout needs to be fast. If you dither, don't assume that your competitors are sitting on their hands. And don't wait until you have arrived at the perfect transformation game plan. Move into engagement and execution as soon as possible so that you can begin to harvest the learnings and make refinements from doing. This is especially important in transformation efforts, which involve sailing out into uncharted waters.

The Cascade must be designed to elicit *high engagement*. No hyperbolic communication events or employee barbeques are going to get the job done. You must carefully construct and orchestrate occasions that are based on the high-engagement and "safe passage" principles that we have been discussing.

And they must involve and engage *all employees*. Successful transformations are all-hands affairs. It is not sufficient to anoint the top few levels of leaders with the essence of the corporate transformation game plan, have them delegate the expectations to those below, and hope for the best at the end of the performance year.

This employee-focused, leader-led process needs to be introduced right after the corporate transformation game plan has been developed and the top three levels of leaders have developed their Commitments to Action. As Figure 6.2 shows, for maximum employee commitment the Cascade approach must not only be leader-led, but its reach must far exceed the traditional communications and training approaches that have traditionally been used to introduce change agendas into an organization.

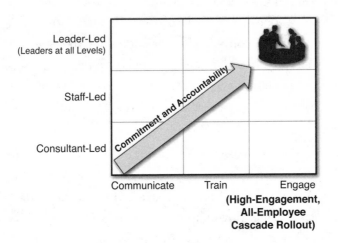

Figure 6.2 The High-Commitment Approach

Let's use a NASCAR-based metaphor to illustrate the transition that needs to take place from planning to employee engagement, alignment, and commitment as a corporate transformation unfolds.[7]

The Transformation Engine

Before introducing the employee supercharger, let's briefly review what management has to do to build the corporate transformation engine. As we so far have discussed, the up-front role of management in launching a corporate transformation involves confronting reality; developing a new Purpose, Strategic Vision, and Business Success Model; and translating that model into a limited set of balanced Transformation Initiatives that are targeted for quantum improvement in one or two years.

The trick is to narrow the focus of transformation down to a few organization-wide initiatives, no more than three or four, that are targeted for quantum—not incremental—change in a short period of time. Such initiatives usually are made up of a mixture of business goals (performance outcomes) and cultural elements (organizational and people enablers).

In addition to focusing the enterprise for quantum change, we have shown that management must articulate the set of Values or principles that people in the organization will aspire to live by, to guide effective decision making and aligned behavior in the envisioned new organization. The process of reinforcing the new values and behaviors is often referred to as the culture change required to achieve the desired business and organizational transformation.

Once this limited set of constructs has been developed and agreed upon by top management and appropriately vetted with other important constituencies, the transformation engine has been built. This is what we have been referring to as "sharpening the strategic arrow before putting all the wood behind it." With the key corporate transformation constructs refined and vetted; the major Transformation Initiatives translated into Areas of Focus, Outcome Metrics, and Action Programs; and the key supporting Values anchored in specific, observable behaviors, management has done its job of articulating the desired future state of the enterprise. The block of the transformation engine has been wrought.

Now is the time to bolt on the employee supercharger.

The Employee Supercharger

Leaders supercharge the launch of well-articulated plans for corporate transformation by rapidly and intensively involving *all* employees in high-engagement Cascades that create understanding, dialogue, feedback, and accountability. These Cascades empower people to creatively align their subunits, teams, and individual jobs with the major Transformation Initiatives of the whole enterprise. If done well, the Cascade events may accomplish their primary mission of refocusing and reenergizing managers and employees by creating an intensive initial experience that can be accomplished in as little as one to one-and-a-half days. The real management challenge is recognizing that they must make such a commitment if they ever hope to engage employees and unlock the value they can add to the transformation effort.

What goes on inside a high-engagement, all-employee Cascade?

First consider a large room filled with all the managers of a major subunit of a corporation. (A similar setting is subsequently created in which all individual contributors in a subunit join their managers for a one-day, all-employee Cascade event and so on down through the organizational ranks, ending with all individual contributors.) Everyone is assembled around round tables of six to eight managers each. Every manager has his or her own "playbook" for the coming year, which contains a series of modules organized around the key corporate transformation constructs: a review of realities, an articulation of purpose and strategic vision, the new Business Success Model, the Transformation Initiatives (one module at a time), and the company values and expected behavior changes.

The Cascade stage is set by the executive leader, who explains the business realities, Purpose, Strategic Vision, and Business Success Model and Values. Then members of the leadership team, who also serve as champions of the Transformation Initiatives, introduce all managers (and in the subsequent sessions, all employees) to each Transformation Initiative, as well as to the aligned company values, using a high-engagement methodology.

Tablework teams are created to enable all managers of a subunit to learn about the vision, stretch goals, and metrics for each initiative before spending time in a dialogue to translate these constructs for meaning and action for their teams and for their own jobs. At the conclusion of each dialogue module, the tablework teams report out their preliminary translations and job-level commitments and learn about those of other teams. Then the tablework teams reconvene to discuss what they have learned. They conclude by drafting a near-final set of team- or job-level commitments to enable them to align their job behaviors with the initiative. The process is repeated until all three or four Transformation Initiatives have been translated for job-level action.

To complete the Cascade process, managers in a subunit conduct a subsequent one-day Cascade meeting with all their individual contributors to delineate job-level commitments that have a clear line of sight back to the handful of organization-wide Transformation Initiatives, as shown in Figure 6.3. Employees finalize such individual business commitments with their supervisors during the following two weeks.

The following two figures are provided to give you a tactical feel for how these compressed Cascade sessions are set up for a one-day format, which is typical for the top several levels in an organization. Figure 6.4 provides an overview of the Cascade macro agenda. The corporate transformation playbook that all attendees are given contains all of the transformation presentations, tablework templates for structured dialogue, and commitment recording forms for quick access. Note that the meeting format is quite compressed to make best use of participants' time away from work, and simple, structured worksheets are provided to keep discussions on track and everyone focused on the task. (Computers and cell phones are banished from the session.)

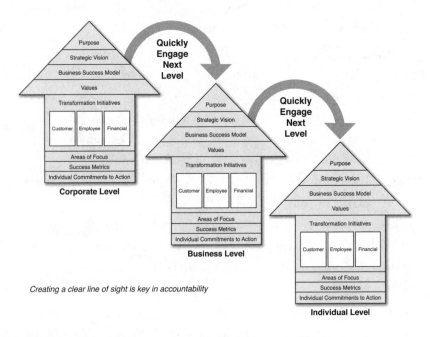

Figure 6.3 Cascading Organization-wide Alignment and Commitment

Multiple departmental teams at the same organizational level are usually assembled together with their supervisors around round tables in a large meeting room for this compressed exercise of learning, dialoguing, and commitment setting. The energy in the room is palpable. Not surprising, the toolkit provided to Cascade leaders at one of our clients explained that, "The agenda of this one-day Cascade event was designed to be ambitious and to provide a sense of urgency to the transformation process."

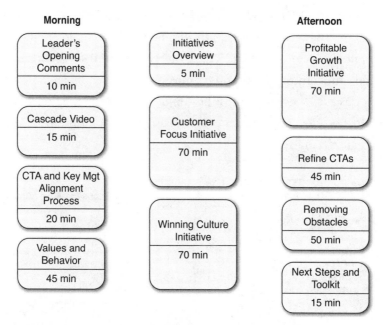

Morning

Leader's Opening Comments
10 min

Cascade Video
15 min

CTA and Key Mgt Alignment Process
20 min

Values and Behavior
45 min

Initiatives Overview
5 min

Customer Focus Initiative
70 min

Winning Culture Initiative
70 min

Afternoon

Profitable Growth Initiative
70 min

Refine CTAs
45 min

Removing Obstacles
50 min

Next Steps and Toolkit
15 min

*As the cascade toolkit of one of our clients explained, "The agenda of this one-day cascade event was designed to be ambitious and provide a sense of urgency to the transformation process."

Figure 6.4 Cascade Macro Agenda

As we have observed through the book, an essential bias in successful rapid transformations is to get everyone in the pool first, with the knowledge that they're going to be headed toward the deep end, before providing all of the training and development needed to make the full transverse of the pool. That is to say, our strong recommendation is to first engage and start the process of learning from executing going and then to follow up quickly with training if needed—but not the other way around. Otherwise, you will risk overloading people and fragmenting their attention. They will simply sink with too much heaped upon them. With aligned and committed employees in the pool, they will be much more motivated to accept opportunities to learn and develop. Another accelerator of transformations.

Finally, Figure 6.5 reveals how the typical Values and Transformation Initiative modules are designed in the rapid, high-engagement Cascade meetings. Given the compressed format, the clarity and simplicity of the corporate transformation game plan are essential to Cascade success. It must be simple enough to easily be translated into job-relevant commitments to action by people and teams at every organization level.

Values and Behaviors (45 min)	
• Presentation	10 min
• BU Leader's CTAs	5 min
• Tablework (Structured Dialogue)	20 min
• Individual Reading of Behavior Change Commitments*	10 min

Customer Focus Initiative (70 min)	
• Presentation	10 min
• BU Leader's CTAs For this Initiative	10 min
• Tablework (Structured Dialogue)	30 min
• Sample Reports	10 min
• Individual Reading of Behavior Change Commitments*	10 min

Submission of preliminary commitments to BU Leader with meeting scheduled within 5 days to review and approve each individual's CTAs.

Figure 6.5 Sample Cascade Modules (One-day Format)

At this juncture, the executive and business leaders have set the transformation game plan, and managers and employees at all levels have gone through a compressed cycle of understanding, dialogue, feedback, alignment, and commitment setting. The accelerated process enables people to use their creativity and job knowledge to take prudent risks at their own job levels to drive the transformation challenge. And it is consistent with the conclusion drawn from more than two decades of field research by J. Richard Hackman, a Harvard organizational behaviorist, that team effectiveness is enhanced when managers are unapologetic and insistent about exercising authority about direction, the end state the team is to pursue. Authority on the means by which those ends are accomplished, however, should set squarely by the team itself.[8]

How the Employee Supercharger Works

The recent experience of a Silicon Valley–based high-tech firm with 5,000 employees and global operations provides a constructive example of how a Rapid, High-engagement, All-employee Cascade works. After top management had spent several months defining where the company needed to go and restructuring it into 14 major subunits, they were able to quickly achieve both subunit alignment and employee engagement by dropping the new direction and key initiatives down through the new business and functional subunits.

The chosen vehicle was a multiday Cascade event in each subunit, which involved all of its employees and was kicked off by the CEO and then passed to the new subunit leader and management team. All managers in a subunit, say the European Sales organization, were brought aboard during the first two days. They were intensively exposed to the new strategic vision, the core Transformation Initiatives, and the values and expected behaviors in the intended culture for the corporation and for their own organization. Then all employees in the organization joined in the last two days of the event. At the end of the subunit's four-day, back-to-back, all-manager and all-employee Cascades, a clear line of sight had been created from the new corporate goals, through the goals of the subunit, down to the job-level objectives of all employees in the subunit. A series of similar events took place in rapid succession in all corporate subunits around the globe. The entire high-engagement process was completed in 13 weeks, including a pilot and a "sweeper" event at the end to catch any employees who had not been in the company to attend their subunit's Cascade. Then all of the Cascade content was transferred to the new-hire orientation program.

The learning from this 13-week global Cascade has led to greater speed and intensity in the Cascade process in subsequent transformation launches at other corporations. For example, for the 16,000 employees in a global professional services company, the all-managers events were streamlined to one-and-a-half days, and the all-employee Cascade events were reduced to a single day each. The entire Cascade process took only six weeks to complete with a nationally dispersed workforce. A similar streamlined process was implemented at a 600-employee fiber optics switch maker in an organization-wide total of three days.

Source: Robert H. Miles, "Beyond the Age of Dilbert: Accelerating Corporate Transformations by Rapidly Engaging All Employees," *Organizational Dynamics*, 2001, Vol. 29, No. 4, pp. 313–321.

The Leader-Led Double Loop

Consistent with the principles that we laid out earlier in this chapter, it is critical that the Cascade be leader-led, not led by internal staff professionals or consultants. Because the general, high-engagement format utilizing tablework modules is the same down through the levels, although more streamlined as job scope narrows, a subordinate who goes through a Cascade with his supervisor is fully qualified and equipped when provided a Cascade toolkit, to conduct his own high-engagement Cascade meeting at the next level with his direct reports, and so on. This double looping of activity of leaders at all levels is illustrated in Figure 6.6. Without this double-loop feature, a Cascade would not be able to achieve the consistent messaging and high levels of employee engagement, alignment, and commitment to be able to achieve breakthrough on the Transformation Initiatives in a short period of time—the hallmark of successful corporate transformations.

When a leader at any level participates in a dialogue with his or her boss and peers and makes commitments, there is a good baseline of alignment and engagement. When that same leader has to stand up and guide his or her own team through an identical Cascade meeting, he or she becomes an evangelist.

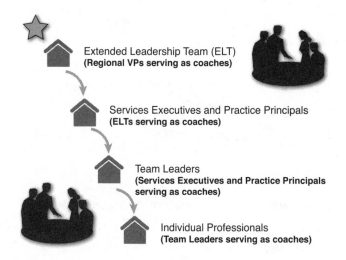

Figure 6.6 High-Engagement Cascade Rollout at IBM Global Services

We have also found it to be quite helpful to conduct Cascade sessions *en masse* at a particular level in a component of the organization. By having such simultaneous Cascade sessions in a large room, it is possible to deliver the same messages about the components of the Transformation Arrow, keep all supervisor-led sessions on the same schedule, and even have a sampling of tablework report outs in the open forum to help everyone see how their commitments fit into the whole.

Employee Responses to High Engagement in Transformation

The responses of employees to the high-engagement Cascade have always been quite favorable. But employees almost always go in to their Cascade events with a healthy mixture of confusion, skepticism, and even cynicism. They expect to witness once again a parade of half-baked ideas from an executive team that is not itself in alignment and that has not taken the time to be clear about what is needed and why or to become committed and accountable for following through for Execution. Instead, managers and employees at all levels tend to leave the high-engagement Cascade with a very different impression of management and level of commitment to the corporate transformation process. Here are a few representative quotes from managers and employees who recently had such an experience during the transformation launch in their company:

> "The Cascade process was nothing short of amazing. It was phenomenal."

> ❋ ❋ ❋

> "I was astounded by the positive impact of the Cascade. We said the very same thing to every single person. It was aligning and motivating, and it produced results."

> ❋ ❋ ❋

> "It was really incredible. In fact, at the end of the day on Sunday when people were told they only had one task left, they actually groaned! It pulled sales and marketing together like they have never been. Then they wanted to know from me how soon manufacturing was going to go through it."

> ❋ ❋ ❋

> "It worked. People got the vision, mission, and values. They got to absorb them and tie them to their own jobs."

> ❋ ❋ ❋

> "It was superb. It was very fast. It was for everybody in the organization. It was focused on a few key things. The focus on 'translation' to relevance for people's own jobs was a key thing in the Cascades."

> ❋ ❋ ❋

"Cascades will remain at the highpoint of their careers for many employees many years later in their careers. Open communication. Minimal hierarchy. Very inspirational."

❋ ❋ ❋

"It was great. It was very well orchestrated. People really worked hard to make it successful. The leaders stepped up to the plate. People left floating on air."

Follow-Through on Execution and Learning

Once the corporate transformation table is set and a clear line of sight connecting organization-level Transformation Initiatives with the job-level, performance, and behavior change commitments of all managers and employees have been established, the whole effort is knitted together by the creation of a learning organization in which early failures and successes may be quickly analyzed and shared with all parts of the organization.

Skill or competency deficiencies can now be engaged more fully in the context of a focused, accountable, and truly motivated system. Employees now seek out training and other competency-enhancing opportunities to be able to meet their new performance commitments. The organization refreshes the entire accelerated transformation process on a quarterly basis by maintaining a process architecture, which consists of the business leader and his or her executive team, the normal line and staff management structure, Transformation Initiative champions, a quarterly cycle of leadership follow-through meetings, and occasional focus groups that tap various parts and levels of the enterprise. We will cover these important elements of the transformation process architecture in the next chapter, which focuses on the Execution Phase.

Cascade as Transformation Accelerator

Given the repeated successes across a variety of service, manu-facturing, and high-technology organizations of the *Rapid, High-engagement, All-employee Cascade*, a few fundamental reflections may be drawn. Such an intervention at the end of the initial corporate transformation-planning phase has the very definite effect of *accelerating* the launch of the entire corporate transformation process. It quickly *aligns* the entire company around a limited set of impor-tant transformation constructs: Purpose, Strategic Vision, Business Success Model, Cultural Values, and Transformation Initiatives. It *engages* everyone at or near the moment of transformation launch, enabling them through a process of structured dialogue to use their untapped creativity to redefine the way they behave and perform at work to uniquely support the transformation effort. It does so *rapidly*.

Cascade as Trojan Horse

The *Rapid, High-engagement, All-employee Cascade* also serves as a Trojan Horse for developing leaders at all levels in the organi-zation. Not only does such a Cascade empower employees to take initiative at their level and help launch the repositioning or revitaliza-tion of an enterprise, it also serves as a fundamental "Leadership 101" intervention for everyone in the organization. Indeed, within the one to one-and-a-half day Cascade event, everyone learns how to effec-tively confront reality, develop a compelling vision and success model, articulate a new set of values and behaviors to guide decision mak-ing, and distill a limited set of Transformation Initiatives to focus the entire organization. In addition, everyone learns how to communicate these constructs in a simple and compelling manner, engage people in structured dialogue, facilitate constructive feedback, and establish personal accountability for the new performance expectations.

What follows the actual Cascade event is a demonstration through-out the remainder of the year about what it means to follow through to ensure execution and to create a learning organization to get better at the things that were right at Launch and to make modifications for improvement in those that don't measure up. Indeed, the whole process of refocusing the organization and reengaging all employees is repeated in a more streamlined manner to launch the second and each successive year of the corporate transformation effort, thereby working these leadership expectations and competencies deeply into the marrow of the enterprise's management process.

Overcoming the "Buts"

Despite all of the positive contributions of the *Rapid, High-engagement, All-employee Cascade,* leaders operating under out-moded notions of the organization-individual relationship can usually conjure up a long enough list of potential caveats to dampen the enthusiasm of all but the hardiest transformation leaders. Among the initial protestations are the following list of favorite fears:

- Managers don't have enough time.
- The organization doesn't have sufficient process skills to pull it off.
- We can't afford to have everyone away from their jobs at the same time.
- We need to get everything right before we launch.
- You can't just drop employees into one of these without getting them ready first.
- It's too much of a hardship for people to travel to remote Cascade settings.

We call the act of moving beyond such reservations the process of "overcoming the buts."

All it takes is for the transformational leader to turn the problem back for creative resolution. For example, executives planning the Cascade of a 500-strong, U.S.-based customer service support department were initially perplexed about how to keep customers satisfied while abandoning the phones to attend their Cascade event. They were told by the CEO to come back with a plan. The response was to inform customers well in advance about the event and its role in enhancing customer service, to have the managers' portion of the Cascade event over the weekend, to augment the services staff the week before and after the Cascade to handle overloads, to bring in skeleton customer services staffers from Asia and Europe to minimally cover the situation, and to have services managers on call from the Cascade site the second two days when their employees were going through the process.

Even though there will always be challenges like this to the use of high-engagement approaches, a creative leadership team can almost always find a way to move ahead. And the payoffs during transformation launches, which often stall during or shortly after lift-off, are tremendous.

It demands that executive leaders use all their creativity to engage employees in more fundamental ways that help them more quickly understand and align with the ongoing process of corporate transformation.

The simultaneous challenges of high employee value and high rates of required change make it absolutely essential that executive leaders develop more accelerated approaches to corporate transformation and more intensive methodologies for engaging, aligning, and motivating all employees; indeed, for creating transformational leaders at all levels in the enterprise.

The collective loss in creativity, passion, and determination across organizations has created one of the most underleveraged resources in business today, our human capital. It is due to a lack of engagement. If you choose not to attend to this critical step of engagement in your transformation, you'll have disinterested employees, great strategy binders that have somehow been misplaced, and mediocre results. By planning for a high-engagement, leader-led Cascade process, you can quickly drive breakthrough results by tapping a resource that is bounded only by the limits of human ingenuity and passion—in other words, limitless.

Tips for Cascading the Engage Phase

- Build the capability to engage in dialogue through a tightly structured *Rapid, High-engagement, All-employee Cascade* process that is leader-led.

- Expect top-to-bottom engagement in a matter of weeks, even for teams of 10,000+ employees, by leveraging the different management levels.

- Keep each level of management in direct dialogue with their teams—don't just rely on communicating broadly to the masses to get the message across.

- Keep engagement focused on the top corporate priorities (for example, Purpose, Strategic Vision, Business Success Model, Transformation Initiatives, supporting Areas of Focus, and Values).

Endnotes

1. Portions of this chapter have been adapted from Robert H. Miles, "Beyond the Age of Dilbert: Accelerating Corporate Transformations by Rapidly Engaging All Employees," *Organizational Dynamics*, 2001, Vol. 29, No. 4, pp. 313–321.

2. Survey by Harris Interactive of 11,045 workers.

3. Kenexa, a Wayne-based provider of solutions for employee hiring and retention. The survey compiles more than 840,000

responses from U.S. and U.K. multinational companies. "Usually, employees hit bottom in the three- to five-year range," said Jeffrey Saltzman, Kenexa's New York practice leader, who helped organize the survey.

4. Robert H. Miles, "Type I Transformation: Repositioning America's Most Admired Utility," Chapter 5, *Leading Corporate Transformations: Blueprint for Business Renewal*, San Francisco: Jossey-Bass Publishers, A Division of John Wiley & Sons, 1997, p. 123.

5. A term coined by Jim Nassikas, who turned around the venerable Stanford Court Hotel atop Nob Hill in San Francisco before developing the award-winning Deer Valley Resort in Park City, Utah.

6. Joe Montana, *The Winning Spirit: 16 Timeless Principles That Drive Performance Excellence*, New York: Random House, Inc., 2005.

7. For more detailed case studies of the deployment of the Rapid, High-engagement, All-employee Cascade, refer to Robert H. Miles, *Leading Corporate Transformation: Blueprint for Business Renewal*, San Francisco: Jossey-Bass Publishers, a division of John Wiley & Sons, 1997.

8. J. Richard Hackman, "Why Teams Don't Work," *Leader to Leader*, Winter 1998, pp. 24–28.

7

The Execution Phase

Over the Hump and Into the Slump

A successful launch only puts a leader at the starting gate of transformation.

Jubilation was in the air shortly after the transformation effort at one telecommunications giant began. The CEO was so thrilled with the problem-plagued company's early-stage success in confronting reality and getting people thinking and acting differently that he began to talk about it in public appearances and in interviews with *Forbes* and the *Wall Street Journal*. There's nothing wrong with savoring little victories, but this leader also began to disengage ever so slightly from his involvement with the transformation process.

Soon, an attitude of "Hey, we're over the hump" crept through the entire company; the intensity and sense of urgency that marked the beginning of the transformation process began to wane. Here was a company entering one of the most competitive periods in its history, and people were lapsing back into a business-as-usual state. The old guard political structures came to life again, and agents of change lost the support and protection they needed to shepherd the transformation through the remaining minefields of execution. The company might have been over the hump, but now it was into the slump. The transformation never got back on track and, eventually, the company was taken over by a larger, more aggressive competitor.

Or consider how another company slid into the slump from what seemed like a safe perch. A couple of years into the transformation process, this organization had broken out of a flat-to-shrinking growth trend. They had successfully shifted from being a company that grew through acquisitions only to one that drove growth internally through innovations from customer-focused business units. The company saw whole new arenas of opportunity on the horizon. With the top leadership and employees at every level fully engaged, the rewards were beginning to flow.

Although they could have doubled up on their bets, they began to hedge and make smaller bets instead. They began to compete by simply putting out revisions of products with a few more features rather than challenging the market with new categories of products or new business models. It was a time when the team could have stretched even further than was possible the first and second years, but instead, the team fell back into cautious, incremental decision making. The slump was under way, proving the maxim that the better the process goes up front, the bigger the risk for a slump.

Bit by bit, the bold moves that had led to early wins and breakthroughs in performance were replaced by hesitation. Management took the lead, delaying difficult decisions. One of the business units was clearly out of alignment with the company's new direction. It needed to be sold, and its resources redeployed in the divisions that were sitting on the new critical path. When management got an offer, it fiddled around before rejecting it. Later, when the leaders finally got serious about what needed to be done, they were able to sell the unit for only a fraction of the previous offer.

Following a great transformation Launch is tough. How can you keep your people energized and focused? As the natural tendency to slump takes root, leaders often look for the next "big thing" to bring the energy back up. At times, they have looked at the ACT process as a planning and launch vehicle, and once the plan is announced and performance management is reset at the front end of the Execution Phase, they are keen to pursue new issues and strategic ideas. So shortly after the Cascade Phase, they drift into adding new programs in search of an answer. But by doing this, they put their organizations right back into the clutches of Gridlock. The system gets overloaded, and people see another flavor-of-the-day program in their rearview mirror. They snap back to the old ways of operating, and progress grinds to a snail's pace.

ACT is really an ongoing process that is intended to be run in recurrent annual cycles as it becomes the backbone of the line management process. There is a natural ebb and flow of energy in a company just as there is in every one of us. It is difficult to stay right at the top of your game day in, day out. And the more you push for peak performance, the more you need to recuperate and recharge the batteries at some point. So how can you make this work and manage the humps and slumps in your continual drive for turning BIG ideas into BIG results?

The best way to avoid the slumps, or really just minimize them, is to anticipate where they will come and design specific interventions at these predictable waypoints into your transformation roadmap to handle them.[1]

Figure 7.1 shows three of the highest-risk Execution slump points.

- *Post Launch*—The first quarterly checkpoint after a full and intensive Launch Phase
- *Midcourse*—The third quarter going into a final push for year-end results
- *Relaunch*—The replanning and relaunch of the next performance year

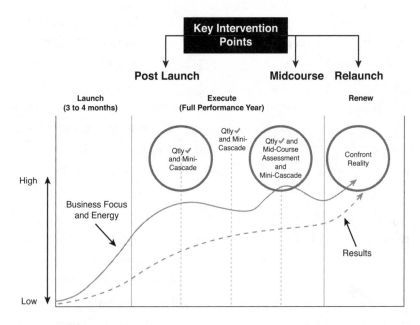

Figure 7.1 Execution Humps

Hump #1: The Post Launch Blues

Gearing up a full organization for a strategic shift or big boost in growth is absolutely hard work. Doing it in a three- to four-month cycle is an all-out sprint. If the organization hasn't been used to speed and high engagement, this can be exhausting. The team will feel a strong urge to sit back following the intensive Launch and Cascade Phases for a moment to take a breather. This is especially true if the initial Launch is successful and a few of the *Quick Start* initiatives have already shown results. We call this execution hump the *Post Launch Blues.* As one executive explained the feeling:

> It is like you've just run a 400-meter, full-out sprint. As you cross what you think is the finish line, you're told, great first lap, but you're actually running a marathon. So, good start, but keep up the pace.

This reaction is normal and expected. After the Cascade work sessions are complete throughout the organization and every person has developed line-of-sight individual Commitments to Action, people really do need to get down to the business of executing what they said they would do. This requires more tactical focus and energy. Sometimes this shift in focus from planning to doing is mistaken as a departure from the new emphases in high engagement and breakthrough thinking back to the "old way" of doing things. And in some cases, that is what happens.

As the day-to-day pressure and grind retake center stage during the first quarter into the Execution Phase, old habits can gradually sneak up on the system. Leaders who were working in a more open and engaging mode can switch back to the command-and-control mode. And priorities set in the Launch Phase will be challenged as immediate expense pressures arise and revenue and other tactical goals have to be met.

At the same time, as the transformation leader, you might begin to feel as though you've done your part in getting the process launched. Because the full roadmap, strategic direction, and transformation initiatives have been launched and cascaded, you may feel that it is now time for the team to simply execute.

But delegation cannot be given over to abdication. With delegation, the leader must stay firmly engaged. He or she must actively champion the Transformation Initiatives and visibly model the new desired behaviors. In their efforts to do this, it will not be sufficient for leaders to simply endorse or preside over these things. There is a saying about the messages of leaders that goes something like, "Just when you are sick of saying it, they are just beginning to hear it."

An extremely smart and creative leader was very much challenged by this dynamic. He had a good ability to converse with people at multiple levels of the organization, he knew the business as deeply as any other person, and he had created communications events in the company to get his message out to the troops on a regular basis. These were all the right things to do. But each time he addressed the organization, he wanted to say something new, insightful, and creative.

And given his sharp mind, he could do that very easily. The challenge, however, was that the team viewed his new ideas as shifts in the transformation game plan. His efforts to stimulate were confusing and defocusing. His intent was to add more dimensions and depth of understanding to the strategy, but by using different analogies and different frameworks for laying out the key points, it looked to others as if he were altering the strategy or the Areas of Focus, or worse, pancaking them on top of existing ones every time he got in front of them.

Ballast and Keel

There is an important dimension of leadership that is quite boring to many creative, hard-charging types. It is serving as the ballast and keel for the company. Ballast is the weight that keeps a ship upright when the winds, waves, or other external conditions try to tip it over, and the keel is used to hold the ship on a straight course. This role of holding the course and keeping things grounded sounds different from the role of a transformational leader, whose job it is to take the company to new heights and get people to break out of old patterns.

Coming off of a high at which the team is energized, focused, and engaged can be confusing for the leader, who needs to switch into the ballast-and-keel role. However, that is just what is needed following a strong Launch because a real transformation is about execution, where leaders at all levels need to have a consistent message. The transformation leader has to set the stage for them to do this down below. Starting each staff meeting during the Execution Phase with a review of the initiatives and progress, individually calling attention to people and plans that have drifted out of alignment, and communicating the same messages over and over are what everyone will see if the leader has effectively shifted into the Execution mode. All of the normal communications channels need to feather into this flow as well. A forewarning to creative Corporate Communications people in the organization: They too will sometimes find it hard to hammer the same message repeatedly rather than put out fresh content at each new opportunity. Therefore, they too need to follow the ballast-and-keel analogy if the organization they serve is going to be able to make the shift from big ideas to big results.

Assuming the leader is able to make the launch to execution transition by staying the course, as the first quarter of performance lifts off, all eyes will be on the leader again.

The half-life for most corporate programs is just about a quarter. So people will be watching to see if this effort has all just been lip service or a flavor of the month, as opposed to something that will last. Some leaders consider the first checkpoint as too soon to really test results, which for some initiatives is true. But it can't be too soon to test whether leaders and all employees are really executing against their commitments to action and living the behavior changes. Those are the real tests of commitment as execution unfolds throughout the performance year.

Company-wide Transformation Initiative Teams

In addition to the conviction and commitment to the plan, there is a need, especially in the early stages, to make sure that the transformation initiatives are fully sponsored and driven from the top. Building traction takes muscle and drive; it is not an automatic part of the process and is why it takes senior leaders up front. The key to building traction with the initiatives is to make sure that they are orchestrated from a performance and learning perspective. On the performance side, they must become a part of the normal daily running of the business rather than be treated as a special program or overlay. On the learning side, there has to be Execution "oversight." Senior executives need to play both roles. *All members of the SLT are Co-Champions of one of the Transformation Initiatives,* and *each SLT member is responsible for driving all of the corporate Transformation Initiatives in his or her part of the organization.* We call this the *Two Hats* of executive leadership, as shown in Figure 7.2.

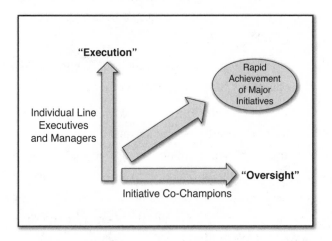

Figure 7.2 The Two Hats of Company-wide Transformation Initiative Co-Champions

The structure for doing this starts long before arriving at the Execution Phase, with the creation of the SLT-level Transformation Initiative Team Co-Champions reporting directly to the CEO at the beginning of the corporate transformation Launch Phase. Their initial job was to bring a cross-functional perspective to the operationalization of their assigned Initiative. With the requirement that all SLT members have a role in shaping these Initiatives and in vetting them with their peers, the ACT-based setup ensured that all senior corporate leaders were engaged in the transformation and that more than just one functional or business perspective would be influential in shaping each Initiative.

For example, charged with developing, say, a people Initiative, a business unit executive would typically co-chair the effort with the head of Human Resources, and those two would walk their Initiative through a series of steps in the ACT process where they would be scrubbed by their peers until approved for rollout during the Cascade and Execution Phases. Moreover, after approval by the CEO and the SLT peers, each member of the SLT would set Commitments to Action, vetted by their peers and approved by the CEO, to drive *all* of the Initiatives in their part of the organization. This much we reviewed in detail in Chapter 2, "Structuring Your Transformation Launch," as part of the structuring of an ACT-based corporate transformation.

With their experience in building the Transformation Initiatives, the company-wide Co-Champions bring aboard their Initiative Teams divisional initiative champions for every major component in the organization just prior to the shift into the Execution Phase. These cross-functional teams are responsible for *execution oversight*, which includes the following duties at company and divisional or department levels: (a) measurement progress against metrics on their initiative, (b) identification of emerging gaps or shortfalls in their execution, (c) collection and sharing of leading practices on their Transformation Initiative across the organization, and (d) communication to all employees of needed refinements and course corrections.

Execution "Oversight"

Often, Senior Leadership Team members and their divisional counterparts are initially confused about what the term execution "oversight" actually means as applied to their role as Co-Champions. What works is to have each set of initiative Co-Champions and their company-wide teams share primary responsibility for overseeing progress on and learning about their assigned Initiative during the Execution Phase. This role is quite different from the particular line management responsibility that each manager has for driving all of the initiatives in his or her area of authority. Quite simply, the burden of driving the execution of all the initiatives should not fall on the

Co-Champions. The achievement of the Initiatives unambiguously remains the responsibility of line and functional managers, who each own in their published Commitments to Action a part of the actions required for success.

So to be doubly clear, the execution oversight duties of a company or divisional Co-Champion are assumed in addition to whatever line or functional management responsibilities he or she might have for achieving *all* of the corporate-wide Transformation Initiatives based on his or her personal Commitments to Action. And none of the other executives and managers are off the hook from having accountability to execute on their part of *all* of the corporate Transformation Initiatives.

Quarterly Leadership Checkpoints

The company-wide Initiative teams have two primary vehicles for getting their jobs done so that line managers, together with their supervisors and individual contributors throughout the organization, can do their best job of implementing the Transformation Initiatives in their sphere of authority and job scope. One is the quarterly, one-day meeting of the Extended Leadership Team (ELT). The other is the Quarterly Mini-Cascade, which we cover later in the chapter. The Mini-Cascade vehicle is essential for getting timely information to everyone in the company on progress and quick refinements in courses of action to accelerate the execution of the corporate Transformation Initiatives. Each department in the company needs to roll out its own Mini-Cascade immediately following the quarterly ELT checkpoint event.

The quarterly ELT checkpoint meeting consists of the CEO, his or her direct reports, and their direct reports; a convening of all of the business and functional departments in the company. The company-wide Initiative team Co-Champions share progress of their Initiative, as well as lessons learned across and throughout the enterprise and needed refinements in a carefully structured and simple format. It should be no surprise that the department teams are organized around tables together so that with their SLT leaders, they can use tablework and structured dialogue to make sense of what they hear about each initiative, translate and prioritize that information for relevance, and develop a plan for informing and reengaging all members of their organization with the rollout of their own quarterly Mini-Cascade.

The way in which each company-wide Initiative team prepares for this quarterly checkpoint event comprised of the top three levels of management led by the CEO is summarized in Figure 7.3.

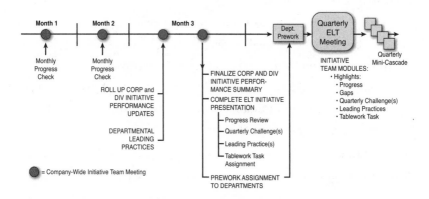

Typical Initiative Team Quarterly Meeting Schedule

Figure 7.3 Company-wide Initiative Teams: Meeting Schedule During Execution

With a well-structured quarterly checkpoint that tests progress and accountability and that reengages the team, new life will be driven into the execution of next quarter's performance. This renews the faith that management will follow through, builds confidence that everyone is headed down the right path, and reinforces the sense that accountability to the commitments to action is real. This becomes the fuel that will drive the transformation forward long after the excitement of Launch.

Hump #2: Midcourse Overconfidence

The next high-risk point for a major slump typically comes after two quarterly checkpoints or so have been passed. Now, at about eight or nine months following the Launch, results are starting to build momentum, and the process itself is very well understood and is being used in many parts of the organization. To return to the sailing analogy, land is dropping out of sight over the transom of the launch vehicle, and a feeling of smooth sailing without need of course corrections can set in. Employees have survived the new language system of the transformation and have mastered its methodology. They ease back into the captain's chair and begin to relax. We call this the *Midcourse Overconfidence* hump.

During this part of the transformation process, there will most certainly be unexpected challenges that have come up along the way and things that aren't working perfectly with your process. Such inevitable challenges and issues become opportunities for those who want out from under the accountability and rigor or want to return to the "good old days" to take their shot.

Sometime after the second quarterly checkpoint, you'll get a comment or email message that looks something like this:

Well, this process has really worked well so far overall, but I think we've gotten the best out of it that we can at this point. The work sessions at the last quarterly checkpoint weren't really as creative as before, and people just don't need to keep having dialogues and tablework. We were just talking about tactical things anyway. Wasn't this supposed to be about transformation? What we really need now to move the business forward is a hit of innovation to break out our performance. Next quarter might be the right time to have an off-site on innovation using a new break-set thinking method I've been reading about. We can shorten up the tablework activities to make room for this. All that discussion is becoming a waste of time anyway. I'll be happy to coordinate the next quarterly checkpoint and really kick it up a notch on innovation.

Loud warning bells and red flashing lights should be going off in your head when you get a request like this. If you don't step up right now to affirm the commitments that have been so carefully put into place, others will help you derail all the hard work that initially got everything focused and moving down the right path. There are good reasons to consider embedding innovation into a transformation effort. This can happen at the times of confronting reality and developing or renewing Initiatives. The main point here is to avoid taking away the drive for accountability and execution that comes from dedicated time to not only present progress, but to get into dialogue to troubleshoot roadblocks and push Execution even faster where possible.

The Process Is Not a One-Time Overlay

Transformations are about launching on a journey of quantum change—not about incremental nudgings or getting to a specific destination and stopping. People in business have become so addicted to considering management interventions as events that they don't initially see a transformation effort as a permanent shift in the basic management process. Many simply expect that any transformation should have an end point at which the next new thing can then be introduced.

One of our SVPs of Human Resources at one of the largest retailers in the world closes the door on the old way of thinking when he prescribes that

Transformations have to be a "never-done" approach. People want to see an end to it so they can go back to "normal." But really living the process of transforming is what has to become the new normal.

ACT becomes the underlying process of the "new normal," and people can feel that they want out at some point because of the discipline and accountability that it drives. The third- to fourth-quarter slump is typically triggered by a sense by opportunists that the year is nearing a close, and the transformation process seems to be drifting down into routine execution activities and tactical actions. But that is hardly a problem with the process. In fact, that is exactly what the process needs to be driving at that point in time. The middle of the performance year is a time to be heads-down, executing the plans. This is hard tactical work. In response, the quarterly checkpoints should be more about eliminating tactical roadblocks to progress that have been identified and looking for ways to accelerate the initiatives at the operating level.

Midcourse Assessment

The key point here is that by the second to third quarter the process will have substantially shifted into a necessarily tactical Execution mode—and that is what it is designed to do. As the "newness" and excitement of the Launch Phase wear off, some people can be expected to start suggesting new methods that are more to their liking and better aligned with their existing skills. Listen for the real process refinements that are needed and act on them without delay. Avoid the temptations to jump to the "next new shiny thing." You don't want your transformation process to ever become "a part of the old way of doing things," so how do you effectively keep it fresh and on the front of people's minds throughout the company?

Because of these predictable patterns, the final quarterly checkpoint of the year—the one at the end of the third quarter—is the perfect point to have a rigorous, multilevel, midcourse assessment of the process itself and transformation progress overall. The idea of the midcourse assessment is to channel any frustrations or shortcomings with the process toward improvements for next year's process. It will always be the case that it doesn't work perfectly the first time through or that it will take some time and practice for it to meld into the way the business is run—the core management process. For that reason, it is important to conduct a deep-dive assessment of the process itself, with no stones unturned and no levels skipped, to obtain firsthand feedback about what's working and what needs to be changed quickly in all jobs and at all levels.

At one company, there was a lot of frustration toward the end of the first year because the high-engagement start to the process had given way during the year to a more command-and-control style of management as pressures drove some executives back into old behavior patterns. The suggestion came up that maybe the transformation process wasn't working and needed to be switched out for something else. As the senior leaders reflected on this idea, they questioned:

How could the simple expectations of having leaders at all levels engage their teams, drive accountability, and follow-through be wrong? They realized, of course, that the process was fine, but that some key leadership skills were sorely deficient and needed to be shored up. So for the next year, they kept with the process but selectively layered in some leadership training and made some leadership changes when they found those who couldn't or wouldn't make the needed changes.

Mini-Cascades

There are many subtle but powerful sources of traction that are available to help a leader sustain forward momentum and guard against the occurrence of a slump.

Beyond the rigorous midcourse assessment, the quarterly leadership checkpoints, and the active championing by the executive leader, there are other ways to help increase traction during transformation midcourse. One that works particularly well is a complement to the quarterly checkpoint meetings of the ELT. You can think of this intervention as the Mini-Cascade, and it takes place at *all* levels of the company on a quarterly basis.

The quarterly Mini-Cascade, which takes the form of a streamlined version of the initial *Rapid, High-engagement, All-employee Cascade*, immediately follows each quarterly ELT checkpoint meeting. The Cascade and Mini-Cascades are marked by the same process of sharing a common view of market and business performance realities, restating the direction, and spending time in working sessions to translate the higher-level plans into refined local actions and accountabilities. Before you jump to the conclusion that these steps might be overkill, consider how simple these powerful interventions can actually be. Put another way, Mini-Cascades are a big deal in maintaining momentum, but they don't have to be treated as expensive, time-consuming, overly produced events. In fact, the more the Mini-Cascades are simply a part of daily operations, the better. Some of the most successful Mini-Cascades have been ones that store managers have organized with their sales personnel around a pot of coffee and a box of donuts just before the doors open to customers or those that field supervisors in a rock quarry have set up for their employees on the tailgate of their pickups.

Regardless of how simple the setting you choose for quarterly Mini-Cascades, the important thing is that they keep everyone, not just the executives at the top, engaged and informed. They bring to everyone in the organization a candid assessment of progress, news about best practices that have been identified during execution, and carefully selected challenges to help accelerate progress at all levels in the company.

By refreshing the entire organization in this simple manner on a continuing basis during the Execution Phase, you also maintain the clear line of sight from top to bottom in the organization that you created with the initial Cascade during the Launch Phase. This makes it easy to spot intermediate leaders between you and the rest of the organization who are actively driving and those who are blocking the forward movement of the effort. In essence, by sticking with the Mini-Cascades each quarter, you continue to reinforce the critical elements of alignment and accountability at all levels. This empowers engaged employees lower in the organization to put upward pressure on alignment, which complements and reinforces what you are exerting from above.

The key to making the Mini-Cascades work is in keeping them simple and focused on conversations with leaders and their teams at all levels, not on administrative forms and checklists. For example, one company was looking to drive accountability to individual commitments on an ongoing basis. For this, they leveraged technology that would allow managers and employees to use a standard Web-based tool to set and track performance. They believed that would give managers an easy way to have ongoing check-ins on performance. But compliance was considered having 100% of your employees' goals input into the system, not necessarily the quality of the goals. As a result, compliance was above 90%, but the goals were not well thought out, and many managers just demanded that people input their goals. They never had an actual conversation with the person either up front or over time. Instead, they relied more on the corporate recording system than on quarterly performance checkpoints at all levels to drive follow-through. Their focus on administrative compliance and on tools rather than meaningful conversations diluted the effectiveness of their follow-through efforts.

In another sample company, they embraced the simple concept of declaring their performance commitments as individuals and as teams, starting at the top and going all the way through the organization. During the first quarter after the initial transformation launch, one-page paper forms that showed the individual team members' goals began to be posted in the hallways around the offices. This wasn't by mandate. One team, which was proud of the challenges they had taken on, posted their sheets in the hallway around their work area. Then the idea of posting caught on throughout the company. During the quarterly performance checkpoints and Mini-Cascades, the leaders talked about how to accelerate things that were already working and how to course correct things that were lagging. The leaders each updated their personal Commitments to Action (CTAs) to reflect needed changes, often electing not to change the original numerical goals, but to shift their CTAs in order to accelerate performance of the initiatives. Each leader would work with his or her immediate team and then on down through the full organization until all employees had been through the Mini-Cascade. These quarterly meetings were not expensive, time-consuming, or overly produced affairs. They were simply the normal staff meetings and tailgate operations meetings that were happening anyway. However, instead of reviewing new policies and discussing other administrative items, they would use one meeting per quarter to focus on performance management at the immediate job level.

Amazingly, employees would update their team and individual commitments, and you'd see a refreshed set of commitments posted in the hallway just a few weeks after the executives reset their priorities and commitments. The resetting at all levels would be in response to challenges and best practices that had been clearly articulated to everyone based on work by the top three levels of leadership at the company's quarterly checkpoint meeting. The role modeling of the executive team, the push to make the commitments real, and the continual drive for improvement are what drove refinements in everyone's on-the-job commitments and performance.

Creating Mini-Cascades that dovetailed right into the normal operations of the organization is what kept the energy and commitment high enough to avoid any major slumps. When the CTAs were posted on the walls, they became a constant reminder of the transformation priorities. When each level of management took time to hold a quarterly Mini-Cascade, it provided an opportunity for everyone at all levels to reengage, recommit, and refocus, which is something that all of us can use at least on a quarterly basis. Quarterly performance checkpoints and especially the Mini-Cascades are often a place where leaders start to cut corners on the process. But just like pulling up short on a golf swing, without the follow-through, you rob the full process of power and greatly increase the chances of an off-target hit. It is the same thing with transformations—to enhance traction for execution, they need every bit of creativity you can muster to keep everyone focused, engaged, and interested.

The ACT-based corporate transformation process that incorporates these elements during the Execution Phase is summarized in Figure 7.4. It emphasizes the need for mini-cascades to immediately roll out after each quarterly checkpoint meeting of the top three levels of management; the same group of SLT and ELT leaders who planned the transformation game plan during the Launch Phase. The figure also reminds us that in parallel to the continued focused on the major initiatives in the corporate transformation game plan, the leadership team must also keep track of important strategic and capability projects under development that were not ready for prime time at the beginning of the Execution Phase, but that may be feathered in to the process when they are ready to go.

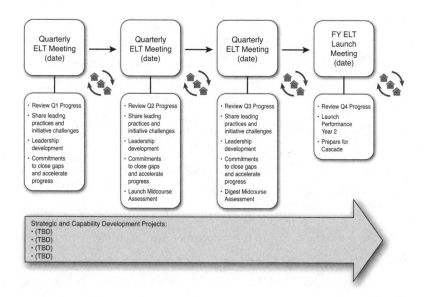

Figure 7.4 Execution Phase Roadmap

Hump #3: Presumption of Perpetual Motion

This brings us to the final high-risk hump. We call it the *Presumption of Perpetual Motion*—the belief that especially first-year success breeds among some executives that since things are going so well, why do we need to intervene? It rears its head right before the end of the first performance year when everyone is trying to figure out what's next. And you know you have a case of it if one of the members of your SLT comes up to you and asks, "We don't have to go through that all over again, do we?" Your only reply must be, "Absolutely!" only in a more streamlined fashion with the wisdom we have gained from year one.

Launching Year 2

The biggest challenge in launching the next performance year, which makes it different from the other two slump points, is the need to confront reality again. But how much of a rethinking of such core transformation constructs as Strategic Vision and corporate Transformation Initiatives do you want to encourage? So much momentum has been built and depth of understanding of the new direction that it would certainly derail progress to scrap everything and start fresh. And it is always hard for the leader and the key executives to work up the energy to go through a full replanning and relaunch cycle. On the other hand, it should also be clear at this point that a lack of regular reality confrontations is exactly what puts most companies behind the eight ball in the first place, so it is always warranted even if difficult.

The key to anticipating and avoiding this slump is to ready the organization for the next full performance year by running it through a complete, more streamlined set of confronting reality, focused alignment, and engagement phases. These are the same phases you employed during the initial launch, only in a more compressed and informed fashion than the first time around. The baseline customer needs, market, and competitive content and process assessments have already been established. But still, take nothing for granted and challenge everything before you finalize the key initiatives for the next year. Moreover, if you did it right the first time, managers and employees will catch you in the hallways and ask you when they are going to receive their playbook for the next year. They'll actually be looking forward to reengaging and recommitting.

Don't disappoint these enthusiastic allies.

The ACT process is designed to be repeated on an annual cycle that looks like the business performance curves in Figure 7.5. Notice that there is some overlap between years where the current year's plans are being executed and the next year's plans are being created. The circles labeled "Annual Refresh" indicate where the steps of confronting reality, focus, alignment, and engagement occur for each successive performance year. By repeating these steps on an annual basis, the ACT principles become part of a more rigorous management and business planning process.

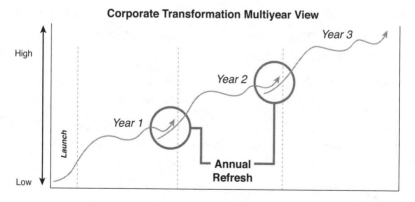

Figure 7.5 Annual Transformation Refreshes

During each annual refresh, running through another round of confidential executive interviews, talking with customers and noncustomers, and reviewing major market trends from an outside-in perspective are all useful ways to confront reality again. It is difficult to know, as an insider, when you have outgrown or overplayed your strategy and positioning. If you shortchange these important steps, you'll miss the shifts in the external environment that need to be factored into your second-year plans. The only way to test for these changes is to be wide open in your confrontation of reality each year.

With all of that said, there is no reason to automatically scrap all of the existing plans and momentum. It is likely that much of a given year's plans will still be valid for the next year. In fact, many initiatives will be, by their nature, multiyear efforts. But inevitably, based on performance and learning the prior year, some of the Areas of Focus and the Outcome Metrics that fall within the key corporate Transformation Initiatives will almost certainly need to be refreshed and refocused.

If a Strategic Vision is strong enough, it should provide a constant pull forward by creating a tension between today's reality and where the company is going. If it is still serving this purpose, keep it as is. If the Business Success Model is still correct and is proving to be a strong competitive advantage, keep it. These elements typically run in longer cycles than a single year.

Transformation Initiatives and corresponding company Values can run in shorter cycles, especially at the level of the specific Areas of Focus for execution within each Initiative. For example, in the case of one retailer, the first year Transformation Initiatives included Customer Focus, Winning Culture, and Profitable Growth. The initial Customer Focus Initiative was aimed at improving the price/value perception customers had of the company, improving customer experience, and establishing the brand. As they entered the second year, there was a lively debate about the most appropriate Areas of Focus for this Initiative for the next year.

The price/value perception had been a surprise as a big impediment to growth for the company. The initial reality confrontation had revealed that customers believed the company had the worst price/value proposition of their competitive set. This meant that in many cases when customers would make up their comparison shopping lists, the company's stores would not be included. For this reason, the merchandising organization hit this issue hard in the first year by putting major programs in place to shift perception and the realities of their pricing strategies. As a result, the company had the competitive gap closed based on external surveys by the end of the first performance year. Revenue growth and higher margins had been achieved, and the company had its highest single sales day in history in that year. So as the transformation initiatives were being reexamined for the next year, price/value perception as an Area of Focus within the company's Customer Focus Initiative was removed. Most agreed with this decision, but some executives were quite concerned that it would signal a relaxation on the pricing issue. In the end, the executive team declared victory on that Area of Focus and agreed that managing competitive pricing would simply become part of the ongoing operational focus and didn't need special attention.

The other two Areas of Focus within the Customer Focus Initiative now needed more attention. Brand positioning had been firmed up by marketing during the previous year and now needed to be rolled out company-wide. The goal was to focus on all customer-facing employees as living examples of the brand itself, which required a full engagement of the organization and focused execution on specifically designing training and programs. Also the work on developing the customer experience Area of Focus in the first year had concentrated almost exclusively on improving the atmosphere of the stores. A more comprehensive approach would be needed for this Area of Focus in year two that would go deeper into product mix, solution positioning for target segments, and more fundamental changes to the shopping environment.

A sharpening of the Strategic Vision in year two to focus more on small business customers dictated that the customer experience should also now be more fully targeted across the store and especially with the sales consultants and service technicians to small business customers. So the two remaining Areas of Focus under the Customer Focus Initiative were tuned up and launched in the second year.

They were given extra attention and resources that would otherwise have been diverted to support the former price/value perception Area of Focus within the Customer Focus Initiative. This example shows how the business initiatives can be reset and stretched at the launch of each new performance year, while maintaining the same overall process architecture for the transformation effort.

Oh Right, the Behaviors...

The root cause of many slumps is often based on a regression in the behaviors and mindsets whose initial changes originally fueled the transformation Launch. Behaviors are more important than the process itself in driving true accountability and execution of a transformation. So often they are considered as an afterthought rather than a primary driver that is integrated into the transformation effort on day one.

From the beginning of the Launch through the first year, all leaders are specifically called on to generate a new operating model and launch a major transformation of the business. They are also asked to commit to and personally model needed behavioral changes that reinforce the transformation effort. As you get to the front edge of year two, the values and the behaviors that were pointed out at the beginning of the transformation as critical to driving the change can easily fade into the background if you are not vigilant. Things are moving forward, so many wonder why they need to continue to worry about the "soft stuff."

Attitudes categorized as the "soft stuff" often include the sense of urgency, a questioning of everything, tough due diligence on yourself, high-quality dialogue between you and your colleagues, fact-based decision making, and other elements that drive an effective confrontation of reality and driving of accountability. As those behaviors slide backward, so does the energy to challenge assumed business realities and all things sacred to the way the business has been run. When this happens, the whole transformation effort can slide back into the grind of safe (versus bold) bets and incremental (versus quantum) improvement expectations.

As the leader, you will set the tone for the amount of energy, rigor, and competitiveness that goes into the process of confronting reality from year to year. The more energy and focus you drive into that process, the greater the organization will stretch. Given the right process architecture, you will always be in a good position to deftly adjust the amount of stretch you and the members of your team are willing and able to take on each new performance year.

You Don't Get to Relax

The common theme you might notice across the antidotes for the three slumps is that there is a huge responsibility on the shoulders of leaders to set the tone for pressing forward.

Some transformers are often so eager to succeed that they exhaust their energy on the planning and launching stages. They do such a great job of confronting reality, focusing their organizations on the critical areas of transformation, and engaging the executive team in the process that they experience a kind of euphoria that leads them to put the crucial next stage of execution and accountability on cruise control. Most are of the old school in which commanders figure everything out and then toss it all over the fence for the rest to get the job done. They rely on the initial excitement and momentum they created to carry the transformation process through to its conclusion. It doesn't work that way. As the leader, you need to always be on your game and particularly alert to the threat of slump and derailment at the three critical points following transformation launch: the immediate post launch slump, the midcourse slump, and the failure to effectively confront reality and relaunch the next performance year.

Plan to Punctuate the Equilibrium Regularly

Without a heavy dose of confronting reality up front every year, a transformation process just becomes a part of the general inertia instead of a way to break away from it. Used correctly, ACT can serve as a process to continuously transform ahead of the market, to reinvent commodity businesses before they lose the ability to generate enough profits to fund the change, to substantially raise the bar and stretch forward continuously, and to become a leader in your business.

The idea is to keep loading bigger and bigger challenges for the organization into the front end of each year, building on previous successes with the same transformation process, which over time will become indistinguishable from what everyone in the organization comes to view as "our management process." By continually taking on larger challenges by using the same, simple, known architecture, your process will become more streamlined and stronger over time. Over time, it should be completely integrated into the normal management process of the company. The strategy will be refined by confronting reality and resetting the focus each year: Budgets and operating plans will be set through the alignment process; individual performance management targets will be set through the development of commitments to action and behavior commitments; and performance will be monitored through the quarterly checkpoints throughout the year. Therefore, you and your team will be able to spend more quality time on strategic thinking, market innovations, and operational breakthroughs, and you will be able to more routinely turn your BIG ideas into BIG results. At that point, there will be no need to have a special name or "campaign" around the process at all; it will just simply be how business is run.

Tips for Overcoming Predictable Execution Humps

- Anticipate the predictable points where slumps occur during the Execution Phase and design specific plans into your transformation game plan to avoid them.

- After a successful Launch, make a clear shift into the ballast-and-keel leadership role by continuing to communicate the same transformation messages and holding the focus firm.

- Rigorously assess progress on the corporate Transformation Initiatives and the process itself at a midcourse point during the performance year to make any required course corrections to accelerate things that are working.

- Be clear that the transformation is a "never-done" process. It is not a one-time intervention, meeting, or event.

- Keep all employees focused on delivering results and accelerating wins through a simple, no-nonsense, supervisor-led quarterly Mini-Cascade process.

- Each year, go through a streamlined version of the same Launch Phase to rigorously confront reality, renew the strategy and business model (as necessary), and realign and recommit the full organization.

- Stay committed to the behavior changes that you made as a leader early in the transformation process to keep the energy and focus up where it needs to be.

- Drive to continuously stimulate and reinforce improvements and breakthrough results; don't just preside over them.

Endnotes

1. For an expanded discussion of the predictable "slumps and humps" during the Execution Phase of a corporate transformation and how to engage and overcome them, refer to Robert H. Miles, "Accelerating Corporate Transformations—Don't Lose Your Nerve!" *Harvard Business Review*, January–February 2010; Reprinted in the "Reinvention" issue of HBR OnPoint, February 2012.

8

Perspectives on Speed and Outside-In

Before shifting from the foundational elements of transformation to some of the most promising disruptive new developments, let's pause to take a closer look at two overarching themes whose absence would undermine an otherwise effective transformation game plan.

Speed Is the New Management Discipline

The first theme is the speed or pace of a transformation. As we discussed earlier, leaders achieve productive speed by *simplifying* the transformation constructs and *compressing* its steps. Unproductive speed, in contrast, often results when a leader commits errors of omission in the design of the transformation game plan, skipping an essential step in the roadmap, or rushing through deliberations without structuring them to ensure efficient, high-quality dialogue. Many times this occurs because the leader simply desires speed for its own sake or because of the feeling of being under the gun to make something happen. So it's important to pause here to take a closer look at the speed dimension in leading corporate transformations.

Get the Train Moving, Now

On any business day in Japan, roughly half the country's 123 million people hurtle to work at 100 miles per hour on the world's fastest trains. That's a distinction envied by other countries but not

necessarily by the 63 million Japanese riding the rails. Efficiently loading the crush of passengers is so imperative to the nation's 300,000
railway workers that white-gloved "enforcers" rush along every platform, shoving and squeezing laggards aboard packed cars.

Let's be glad no such enforced mania is needed or even effective for success in corporate transformation or strategy execution. To
put a large organization in motion, what matters is to get the train
moving the right way down the right set of tracks quickly. When that
happens, you will be truly surprised to see how many people climb
aboard before it leaves the station! The right people will get on right
away. Those who want to make the trip but were thinking they might
be able to postpone it until a more convenient time will step on as well
to see how things unfold during the first few stops ahead. Those who
are uncertain about whether they want to go in the new direction will
have to make up their minds. At some of the next few stops, some will
get off because, after a closer look, they've changed their minds!

Forward motion gets both intellectual and emotional attention. In
one sweep, it signals intention, purpose, and commitment, as well as
the direction in which the organization is laying its new tracks.

Speed is a key enabler of success in transformations and strategic
shifts. But it has to be the right kind and pace of speed. *Productive*
speed reinforces decisive action, which helps generate interest and
energy and accelerates the realization of early returns and, ultimately,
breakthrough results. Unproductive speed shows up as frantic flail-
ing, lots of skipped steps that produce a lot of activity, but no breakthrough results.

If you watch Olympic speed skiers, the fastest athletes make it
look effortless. They are relaxed, yet focused. They carve deep, wide
turns that are perfectly timed to put their shoulder just at the edge
of the gate where they turn. By the time they start their run, they
have already visualized their entire journey to the finish line multiple
times so that when on the race course they can anticipate almost every
twist and turn. That is how they achieve speed. Amateur skiers can

be seen bombing down the hill with rooster tails of snow flying up around them, out of control; plowing over flags as they career down the mountain.

The same principles apply in business but are not well understood. In fact, the key elements that create real speed, such as planning your route, developing a routine, staying calm, and thinking through the challenge before taking it on, are often believed to slow down the business. As a result, leaders shortcut these steps and don't take time to do strategic planning, focus and align the team, and engage employees. They may think those kinds of processes are all bureaucratic and plodding—that it is better to just start doing something. There is a balancing point in all of this. But the average leadership team spends far too little time in preparing to run at top speed, and, hence, they operate handicapped, running at a frantic pace with a lot of wasted energy. A retail senior executive with whom we have worked was challenged with running his team like a start-up within a global multibillion-dollar company. He explained the need for speed to his team this way:

> Speed is a choice, and it is a competitive advantage. A transformation process provides a vehicle to accelerate change. It can be a ritual like a pre-shot routine, not a rut.

People make excuses that there is no time for strategic planning or for having a dialogue with the team to prepare. As a result, they leave the starting line of strategy Execution without having a plan—without a visualization of what they will encounter when they try to execute. Others throughout the organization don't understand what they need to do and, therefore, can't anticipate the right actions. Instead, they have to sit and wait for a succession of orders to come from the top. The system slows down as a result. The leaders get impatient and start demanding more of a "sense of urgency," which only serves to intimidate the team and make them second-guess their decisions even more. The team tenses up and becomes unable to solve problems for the obstacles they encounter. That causes the system to slow down even further. Then the leaders start to micromanage everything, the top performers get frustrated and leave, and you are left with an organization of "yes-people" who wait for each new tactical change order from above. This doesn't work.

At the other extreme lie traps of analysis-paralysis—studies and projects that never end and data that are never quite enough or sufficient for some management teams. They just can't seem to put a fork in it. The results, ironically, are just about the same as in the opposite extreme. As leaders stay far removed from the operations, up in their offices in deep contemplation over what to do, forward movement grinds to a crawl, talent exits, and those who remain drag themselves to work day after endless day waiting for some change for the better. In between these extremes lies the *productive* kind of speed that has invigorated the transformation and strategy execution efforts that succeed.

Benefits of Productive Speed

Getting to effective business results faster is, of course, the major goal of applying speed. And as it turns out, it's not just about getting the same results faster; it is getting to better results faster. That is the payoff of *productive* speed. In our experience, as you increase the pace, shorten the decision cycles, and accelerate the alignment and engagement processes, the greater your results will be. Now, we're willing to concede that eventually there might be some natural limits to these effects of increased speed. It's just that we haven't encountered them yet!

The reason results get better is that speed reduces unproductive dithering; it doesn't allow time for dysfunctional political positions to crystallize. It avoids overanalyzing and, more important, overengineering solutions. It shifts the emphasis to a learning-from-doing mode, which enables leaders to achieve results and continue building on that success to reach even further goals.

Not long ago it was believed that strategic plans should be ten years long (about the span of a typical CEO's tenure during those days), and that it would take multiple years to launch a transformation and turn an organization. But since then, many forces have conspired to dramatically accelerate the cycle times within organizations and the markets in which they compete. Perhaps the most profound and prolific influence on speed—the cycle time of execution—has been technology. As companies began to use an earlier version of the ACT methodology on the West Coast during the build out of the high-tech sector, the executives were quite appreciative of the tools for focused alignment and rigorous execution. ACT's simplicity was for them indeed on the other side of complexity.

But the new wrinkle was that they all wanted to do these things in much less time. As they explained, the cycle time associated with their high-tech product development as well as the changing needs of their customers was a fraction of the big metal-bending and paper-pushing enterprises of the past. As time has progressed, another derivative phenomenon has unfolded. The ultimate diffusion of high technology across all sectors has caused companies in all industries and of all shapes and sizes to become more capable of operating on a faster cycle. The "need for speed" has become ubiquitous across industries. The upgrades in the ACT methodology spawned by the high-tech sector have become useful to all industries, with fewer and lighter steps involving a more rapid launch pace to execution.

Other pervasive forces have also been at work reinforcing the need for speed. Not the least of which at the corporate level has been the increasingly heavy push for takeovers. To put it bluntly, if you take too long to improve your business, an impatient activist investor just might get the job done for you! Rapidly expanding global competition, increasingly fickle customers, and just-in-time supply chain management are combining to drive the pace even faster today. To thrive and even survive today, executives need to be able to drive rapid cycles of improvement in their company strategies, business models, and operations.

All Aboard at Internet Speed

This brings us to the CEO of a successful technology company that hit a much unexpected problem during the Internet boom. The CEO had transformed the company from a niche software player to the second-largest retail software vendor behind Microsoft. It was an exciting time.

Given all its success, it was hard to believe that the company was experiencing difficulties. But revenue growth had flattened, and several attempts to identify fast-growing businesses for acquisition had come up empty. As a result, the stock price had lost more than half its value. Worse yet, the war for talent had start-ups enticing the company's star players with huge stock-option deals. Talented people were jumping off the train in growing numbers. Many literally jumped into new BMW convertibles supplied by their new employers. Something had to be done—fast.

The CEO and his senior executives had an impressive track record. They had built companies from scratch, created breakthrough products, and led teams with a passion for new technologies. But the company now felt slow, plodding, and not very inventive. Every day, the *San Jose Mercury News* profiled the latest wunderkinds. Fresh-faced engineering geniuses were ramping new businesses up and down Route 101. The CEO and his executives had no intention of sitting idly by, watching their company flounder.

They began by confronting their current reality. The company had grown by acquiring software makers with strong products but poor distribution. Its solid relationship with retailers helped give a quick boost to the lagging sales of companies it acquired. But within a few years, though, few companies were left for the company to buy. Still the dominant player in its market, it lacked the means to jump-start growth. New markets had to be identified.

A separate problem revolved around the company's structure. It had developed into a fairly loose collection of eight business units representing previously independent companies, each with its own product line. Little collaboration took place; in fact, the BUs often sniped at one another. To counter this feudal system, the company reorganized, coalescing into three highly focused, customer-centric business units. The three executives selected to run these units were chosen for their presumed ability to lead large, complex teams, generate growth, and boost new product development. Most important, they were viewed as both individual leaders and team players.

Obviously, the new arrangement left several of the old business unit heads out of key leadership positions. Some of them—former chief executives of acquired businesses—were more comfortable leading small teams with no corporate oversight. In short, they weren't the kind of general managers the company now needed, and they soon departed. To use the train analogy, the company was finally positioned on a specific track and was starting to move in the right direction. The "wrong people" knew it and got off the train just in time to allow for a smooth departure.

It was shortly after the reorganization that the CEO was able to assemble his new Senior Leadership Team. They agreed on a strategic transformation for the company using the ACT methodology. It would no longer focus on silo products; it would be a customer-driven company with the spotlight on solutions. To kick off the first year of the new company, they vowed that customer research would get as much attention as technology research. By understanding customer needs, the company would begin to create its own innovative products rather than just look for ways to acquire them. And while the market for retail software would remain a core piece of the business, growth would also come from moving into corporate markets. Above all, the leaders were compelled to become brutally honest about the challenges their organization faced. In the end, they embraced a plan to take the company down the track they had laid together. With growing enthusiasm, they urged managers to step forward and speed the train to the next destination. They named their corporate transformation process "Taking Charge."

The new corporate transformation game plan put the company on a new path that kept gifted people in the company, eased out those who didn't fit into the new strategic plan, and attracted newcomers with more of the right talents. Within two years, the shift toward corporate customers had become a significant part of the company's business.

Some people counsel that everything must be perfectly prepared for any kind of launch, with the strategy aligned and all the right people in the right positions. But many leaders who follow that advice find themselves shunted onto the side tracks, still waiting to fire up the engine as competitors and the market landscape roar by and employees leave to find more stable berths upon which to build their careers.

Moral to the story? Preparation is important but not at the expense of motion.

Perhaps the most important reason to get moving is that every day of action accelerates the cycle of organizational learning and adaptation. Movement starts the learning process that must precede any necessary adjustments and refinements, which, in turn, increases your chances of besting your competitors. Cultures that are focused on execution aren't likely to let problems fester for years. In these cultures, the moment a solution is envisioned, it is put into play. If it proves to be faulty, it is just as quickly jettisoned and harvested for things learned to apply to the ongoing business.

In short, early motion starts a learning process and triggers a kind of self-selection. The wrong people either verbally identify themselves or through their actions become clearly visible as misfits in an aligned, high-engagement environment, at which point they withdraw voluntarily or are excused. Meanwhile, the right people step up their performance a notch. Sometimes, totally unexpected individuals suddenly become leaders, and they are much more easily recognized in an aligned and engaged organization. In almost every case, the train builds enough momentum to get the team motivated and enough early success to build on for the big win.

In reflecting on the transformation experience of a global retailer, the president and COO recalled that one of the most important benefits was being able to see new leaders emerge from the ranks. Most of the executive team had tenures of 10 to 15 years, long by today's standards. The organization had struggled in recruiting outside talent and in making decisions about top team members who might not have been in the right roles for the new market requirements. But continued waiting to get the right people on board was not getting the team anywhere. They had to get the organization in motion—no more waiting.

As the company began to move from a pure operations focus to a market-centric approach, it became clearly uncomfortable for many of the leaders to make the shift. At the same time, natural leaders who had before not been exposed to the senior team in terms of their strategic thinking and leadership had the chance to interact more directly with the executives. Within the top three layers of management, individuals with talents in strategic planning, process design, and customer research began to shine. These were skills the company did not think it had, and it was a talent resource that was completely overlooked. By getting things in motion, these individuals were able to jump on board quickly, take leadership roles in helping the organization make the shift, and took the seats that others, by title, should have taken. For the president, the ability to get the train moving first and then use that motion to sort out the right people to keep was invaluable.

The Discipline of Productive Speed

Organizational speed is something that absolutely can and should be managed better. The keys to creating speed are counterintuitive to many leaders. *Productive* speed is achieved when the right kind and amount of process architecture is put into place to stimulate rapid, but deep, decision cycles in management working sessions and ongoing performance checkpoints that drive true progress, not simplistic tactical improvements. But be sure to keep center stage the need to build speed through *simplicity* and *compression* in your corporate transformation game plan, roadmap, and events. Speed achieved through careless omission of an important step or design element will have the opposite effect on transformation success.

Taking time to enter into meaningful dialogue with your team can also seem like a luxury that your limited schedule won't allow. However, leaders eventually discover that shortcutting dialogue to get to faster action only leads to confusion in execution, where debates are repeatedly revisited, problems are dealt with too late, and, hence, big decisions that could create profound breakthroughs are avoided. Leaders who have mastered the ability to drop in the zone with their teams and get deeply into issues quickly have discovered new levels of clarity, focus, and speed in taking decisive action, which, in turn, gets them to bigger breakthrough results faster—and isn't that what we really want from *productive* speed?

The Outside-In Perspective

The other overarching theme in transformation work is a perspective that all leaders must keep at the forefront of their transformation. We call it the *Outside-In Perspective*.

A successful corporate transformation always begins with a true confrontation of reality; one based as we shall see on an "Outside-In" perspective of the business, in addition to the internal view from the team. You need to look at your situation through the eyes of customers and competitors. Their reality is yours.

On the Outside Looking In

The best way to generate an outside-in perspective is to, well, go outside. Get outside of having conversations with the internal team in the same old setting. One company's method was to hold executive strategic planning sessions away from the corporate headquarters in less-traveled cities around the country where they had a market presence. The idea was to spend some time together as an executive team while competitively shopping the competition and making unscheduled visits to their own stores as if they were customers. Such visceral experiences go well beyond what you can get from a PowerPoint presentation of an internally generated competitive analysis or a report by a market research house. Those analyses are useful as well, but they lack the real-world impact of firsthand experience.

However, getting a group of executives together to spend time looking at the market is harder than it sounds. One corporate strategist and prior CEO of a start-up software company, with whom we have worked, points out the challenge. His observation is that there are two types of people you are trying to bring together when you get an executive team together for a strategic outside-in look at the business. And both types of people have valuable views. He explains,

> It's like going up for a ride in a helicopter. The strategists say, hey can we take this thing even higher to see way beyond the fence lines? And what do you think is just over that hill? While the operators go up briefly, have a bigger view, and then say, that was nice...now let's get back on the ground where we belong.

It is the challenge of balancing those two views and making the work useful in driving real decisions that makes the difference in an effective confrontation of reality.

One of the more creative ways of confronting reality that worked well for both types of people occurred in the transformation of a large, highly unionized U.S. utility, which launched a transformation while annually making $1 billion in net profits. The prospect of being able to actually pull off a major transformation of a company initially doing so well and hemmed in by overlays of complacent managers and union work rules was an extremely challenging situation.

Send Employees Out

A creative mid-level executive was given the task of jump-starting the transformation. The biggest challenge he inherited was finding a way to get people motivated to get engaged in the process. His initial instincts were on the mark. He had to get managers and employees at all levels to understand the need for transformation and to leave their comfort zones. They would need to not only support, but actively lead the effort in their areas of responsibility. He first had to get every-one—managers, union leaders, and employees—to confront reality.

The competitive landscape confronting this large, staid utility was becoming occupied not by just the large, traditional rivals, with their heavy overheads and long investment horizons, but increasingly by agile new competitors. New independent power producers (IPPs) were beginning to cherry-pick the utility's highest-margin industrial customers. In addition, escalating deregulation of the electric utility industry was opening up the local market to all sorts of new com-petition from former regional monopolies and independent power brokers.

At one plant location, the urgency of the new reality had become clear to all. Employees at this location could climb to the top of the cooling tower, look out toward the horizon, and see the facilities of two large industrial customers that had been lost to new competitors. But for the vast majority of employees, the need for transformation was not as clear.

The executive's gut told him that the best way to serve up the new reality would not be from the work of consultants or staffers. Instead, he commissioned diagonal-slice teams, made up of executives, managers, union officials, and rank-and-file employees, to go out and engage with the new business realities. These diverse benchmarking teams researched, toured, and analyzed the operations of several large, rival power generation operations. They scrutinized the capabilities of the new IPPs. Indeed, many of the team members were initially puzzled by the fact that the new rivals would open their doors and books to them. During one of the first visits to one of these new, independent rivals, they asked why the company would be so open to a conversation with a competitor and were astonished by the response they got from its executive leader. He replied,

> You guys are like a big aircraft carrier, and I'm a PT boat. You're too big and too cumbersome. You've got too much bureaucracy to turn that thing around as quickly as you need to turn it around. There's a new war that we're fighting, so I'm not concerned about you being a competitor.

The arrogance that IPP executives thought they could beat proud old Southern Company "in its own backyard" was convincing evidence for the benchmarking teams that significant change was not only needed, but essential. As our mid-level executive recalled,

> What they saw blew their socks off because they discovered a totally different approach to the power generation business. They found the IPP plants well built, efficiently run, and, most important, focused on providing low-cost energy. The competitive spirit, employee empowerment, cost focus, lean staffing, and work culture of these new competitors convinced the teams that fundamental, not the usual incremental change was required at [the company].

To complete the confronting reality phase, the executive had the teams develop their own reports and present them directly to the electric power generation employees, thereby completing the team members' ownership of the new reality while disseminating it in a credible way to everyone else.

Within two years, the utility had successfully completed the first leg of its transformation. Its managers, supervisors, and first-line employees were becoming comfortable with their new vision state, it had eliminated hundreds of millions of dollars in overhead, and it had hammered out a "new deal" with its unions to support a more flexible and cost-effective work system.[1]

Talk with Customers and Noncustomers

Seeking the opinions of customers as well as noncustomers is another important way to constructively confront reality. At one high-tech company, there seemed to be no shortage of issues being raised as the new CEO arrived. It was crisis mode, and there were lots of opinions on what was wrong. The sales team, in particular, had significant complaints about the product team's slow pace of new product development. In their view, that was the reason they had lost one of the company's largest customers, which, in turn, had driven the tailspin in revenue. The sales team claimed to be the voice of the customer and expected that view to be given heavy weight in the reality top management took into consideration when making key decisions.

The sales team argued that salespeople are on the front line with customers every day. "We know our customers very well, and they let us know what they need. Nobody in headquarters has that view of reality." Although in general, it is true that salespeople are closest to customers in terms of interaction, they also are likely to get a distorted view on what the customers really need. The nature of the sales-client relationship will tend to lead to discussions about features and price—not necessarily other areas such as the quality and integrity of the salespeople themselves, major new product line ideas, and supply-chain challenges. Sensing that the issue wasn't as simple as that of recent delays in product launches, the CEO embarked on a global tour to meet the company's customers himself.

Salespeople around the world geared up by preparing presentations for the CEO to make to their customers and setting up briefing meetings with them for the CEO. However, the CEO quickly put a stop to that activity and let the sales team know that the purpose of the conversations was not to pitch, but to listen. One of the first visits was to a large customer they had just lost. The CEO went in with no PowerPoint deck and no hard agenda—only with an agenda to find out what had gone wrong. The CEO had the sales relationship manager bring only a blank tablet to take notes. They were definitely uncomfortable in that role. By the time the meeting was over, they had heard about many issues, not the least of which were problems with the sales team's handling of some serious product quality issues. The executives at the customer company commented that they had never had an open-ended meeting like that with a vendor and were shocked that the CEO and his team really just listened.

In addition to talking with all customers, the CEO and his sales reps also conducted interviews with noncustomers, or companies who bought exclusively from competitors. Often, it is uncomfortable to go talk with customers with whom you have not been successful with your sales efforts. However, they are quite often great sources of reality for you. They have nothing to lose by making suggestions for improvements and nothing to gain other than helping another potential vendor keep the market competitive—which is in their best interest. In this case, the noncustomers had the same suggestions as those of the large customer they had lost.

With notepads full of shots of reality from customers and noncustomers, the CEO returned to the office prepared to net out what internal people thought, what different functional groups thought, what customers thought, and what noncustomers thought. Among all of those points of view was reality.

You Are Here: Map the Market

Two of the most useful tools in figuring out how to get to where you want to go are having a map of the area where you are and a big red arrow saying, "You are here." One of the toughest jobs in quickly confronting reality is to create a consistent structure to capture all of the various points of view and pieces of data in one way. Too often, there are competing views all presented from different and often too narrow perspectives. It becomes impossible to net out any sense of reality. Segmentation schemes are different, product groups and market sizing cuts are different, and, at times, even the internal operating data is inconsistent across groups as it comes from various systems all geared to a different structure. Creating a market map is an essential tool in confronting reality.

One example illustrates well the high-level use of market maps. As the music industry was opened up by the forces of the Internet, a number of companies created a market for portable devices to store and play back digital copies of songs stored on your computer and downloaded from the Internet—MP3 players. The service, Napster, opened up the market by creating a capability on the Web for anyone to share their music files with anybody else in the world at no cost. The Napster content was all available online and easy to download so that all the early MP3 devices needed to do was synchronize with a PC, store the music files on the device, and play them back. A host of technology-oriented companies worked to perfect their products for this market, looking only at the customer needs for their portion of the solution. Figure 8.1 shows the initial, narrow market view that set the competitive landscape for the hardware players in this market. As the market matured, they subsegmented the early users of this technology into college students, athletes, and others. Realistically, all of the early customers were gadget geeks of some sort, so when talking to them about their needs, the feedback was the same across customers—faster speed of synchronizing to the PC, more storage, and better playback time or battery life. That's what the companies were hearing, that's what they did well, and so that is what they delivered.

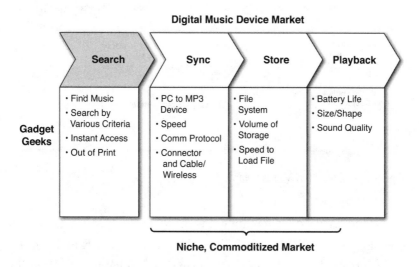

Figure 8.1 Narrow Market Map View

This narrow focus on just providing hardware devices and competing on technical feeds and speeds started to give way when Napster was effectively stopped from letting users share their music for free. Now, an online music source of songs wasn't a given. By that time, people who had never used Napster, because they viewed it as a legal or moral issue, began to see the benefits of online music.

Apple looked at the total customer needs of the broader potential that extended beyond the hardware. They considered a large group of customers who wanted the entire experience and concept of having your entire music library in a small and mobile device. These new people were "noncustomers" as far as the traditional gadget geeks were concerned. But there were a lot of these noncustomers, and they were actually quite willing to buy legal copies of online music, wanted an easy way to manage the online experience with the device, and wanted a great-looking and great-sounding product. Figure 8.2 shows the broader market map and customer needs.

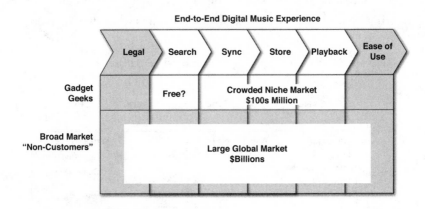

Figure 8.2 Expanded Market Map View

Apple focused on creating the most easy-to-use, legal, music download site on the Internet. They also invested heavily in the design and controls of their device. By focusing on developing a full and finished solution rather than a tech gadget that required a lot of downloading of special software and tinkering, Apple opened up a whole new market, drove better pricing, and came to dominate the market. Apple solved for the needs of the broader market and turned a niche technology device market into a new music distribution channel.

It is easy to get so focused on competing in your narrow space that you ignore the way your customers fully experience and use your product. You can also become blind to entire segments of customers who would use your product if the solution were just a little more complete. You might ignore moves by players that you don't view as direct competitors because they don't appear to be in your space. The market map is a very useful tool for forcing a customer-oriented view of your strategic landscape where you play.

A market map is simply a two-dimensional chart that typically has a full set of categorized customer needs on the horizontal axis and one of several categorizations for the vertical axis, for example, customer segments. Each axis can have a drill-down of detail, allowing for high-level views for strategic planning that can be driven into detail for setting operating tactics. The map forces a customer view of the world, which is where breakthrough ideas come from, and drives a discipline into strategic planning to make more intentional market moves rather than just a collection of random creative tactics.

The executive who earlier described the "helicopter" ride explains,

It is one thing to say you are growing from $1 billion to $2 billion in revenues. It is another to say how you are going to get there. Creating a market map requires rigorous work to get the right segmentation and customer needs model, but once you have it, your ability to find yourself on the map and decide clearly where you want to go becomes easy. And it is not just finding yourself, but clarifying how you'll move forward that is so powerful. It becomes something like the old game of RISK where you have a map of the world and play to capture all territories. To win, you have to carefully decide how to deploy your resources to not only win, but also to defend your territories over time without getting spread too thin.

With the market map in place, the data, such as customer needs, segmentation, market size and growth, competition, product portfolios, service offerings, and R&D investments, are all plotted on the exact same map. The market map then becomes a view that is continually enriched as more data and points of view are generated in your confrontation of reality. Viewing the market from a market map perspective also allows you to force a broader view of the market as you start with customers' overall needs rather than just a view of what you already provide. This releases you from using the current organizational structure (for example, product groups, divisions, services teams) as the main view of the world, which is limiting.

With this simple construct, a single view of your markets, and the data categorized, you have the information simplified into a format that enables efficient, structured dialogue around a limited set of strategic questions, such as the following:

1. Which segments are driving the most revenue size and growth for the market in the future?

2. Which customer needs areas are underserved?

3. Where do we have a true advantage in serving those underserved customer needs?

4. What moves are competitors making that we should either block or avoid?

5. Where should we place our bets on the map, which will indicate what customer needs should be served, what segments we'll target, and how we'll compete?

By paying careful attention to keeping the right pace in the corporate transformation and ensuring that it begins and continues with the Outside-In perspective in mind, leaders will be able to infuse their process with reality and keep enough tension between what could be possible and what they are currently doing to sustain the high levels of energy and focus essential for success. Both are critical dimensions of an effective transformation that is able to achieve breakthrough results in record time.

Now, in the next chapter, we explore some of the potentially disruptive approaches that are emerging, which have the potential for enhancing acceleration and enabling organizations to bottle their transformation experience and convert it into the ongoing and sustainable agility competency.

Tips for Incorporating Speed and Outside-In Perspectives

- Get the train moving quickly.

- Get a grip on the meaning of "productive" speed and how to facilitate it.

- Use *simplicity* in content and *compression* in process, not omission, as the ways to accelerate your transformation.

- Remember to identify Quick Start initiatives and generate early wins even before the full transformation planning process plays out.

- Preschedule all working sessions through the Launch Phase and through all quarterly checkpoints for at least one full performance year following Launch.

- Spend time to creatively look at things from customer, noncustomer, and competitor perspectives.

- Expand your perspective on the market opportunities to reach into the full end-to-end needs experience around your products and services and how that fits into making their lives better.

- Get your employees outside the organization to see firsthand what's really going on with customers, competitors, and your broader business ecosystem.

Endnotes

1. Robert H. Miles, *Leading Corporate Transformation: Blueprint for Business Renewal,* San Francisco: Jossey-Bass Publishers, a Division of John Wiley & Sons, Inc., 1997, pp. 83–126.

9

Building Transformation Traction

Traction in corporate transformations is built both through sound process architecture as well as one-on-one leadership. Just as we have discovered in the crafting of an ACT-based transformation Launch, there are a number of subtle but important micro-levers that a leader can throw to increase individual commitment and build and sustain traction during its Execution Phase. Among these available levers are public commitments, closed-loop accountability, declarations versus promises, ground truth, and the creation of an internal transformation Process Support Team. Each lever may be deployed to add value to your transformation and to speed up its execution.

Building Traction Through Transformational Leadership

We all know it; the Achilles' heel of any effort to shift direction is the ability to build traction by following through. The critical path to achieving breakthrough results is always encumbered by diversions and distractions that have the potential to cause the initially committed to wander off the path. The basic mechanics to follow through are well understood. Set goals and use metrics to track progress, keep your priorities in check, follow up on progress, make timely adjustments, and so forth. It is all so simple, but how many of your New Year's resolutions do you keep? How often do you think of them after declaring them at the beginning of the year?

It's unnatural for many of us to doggedly follow through on things we say we will do. In fact, it is so difficult that the CEO of one of America's leading university hospitals pointed out, "If you look at people after coronary-artery bypass grafting two years later, 90% of them have not changed their lifestyle."[1] So even when our lives are on the line, it is tough to follow through with changes to which we know we need to stay committed.

How can you break that cycle of setting goals and ignoring them until setting new ones again when you realize you haven't followed through? Let's start with something everyone can understand. When you set out to transform your body and health, you commit to working out. What are the ways you use to follow through with that? You tell others what you intend to do and, therefore, publicly commit, you put a plan in place to get into a routine, and you get a workout partner or personal trainer (aka a professional nudge). Not surprisingly, the same things can hold true for leading your business from BIG Ideas to BIG Results.

Commit with Confidence, Publicly

Following through on a plan is directly correlated to the amount of investment and commitment you make up front to build your own confidence in the plan. If you and your team spend one afternoon, or maybe just a long flight on a business trip, developing a strategic vision and creating some corporate goals that sound good, how confident will you be that the plans are right? Not very. In fact, you'll know in your gut that the ideas were quickly put together off the top of your head and are not rooted in any real analysis and strategic thinking. So now, what will happen when results are not building as quickly as you hoped and a new "silver bullet" idea is pitched up for growth? You'll likely jump at that new idea and scrap the old plan. There will be no confidence and conviction in the existing plan to see it through. Some flexibility is fine, and many midcourse adjustments will be necessary, but it is the constant switching, layering on, and dropping of initiatives that causes confusion, Gridlock, and lack of accountability.

With any long-term plan, there will be ups and downs in the results, and you need to have a strong enough conviction in your plan to stick through the small cycles. Of course, there are also the larger cycles when full-course corrections might be necessary. You will address those with regular doses of confronting reality, which are best done on an annual basis or when major industry events occur. But it is the daily, weekly, and quarterly shifts and pressures that can cause organizations to blow too much with the shifting winds. What do you need to do to boost your confidence in your strategic plans? The steps of engaging your team to confront reality and then setting a strategic direction that is rooted in customer and noncustomer input, field perspectives, and a sound business success model are a great start to building confidence in your plan. Conducting a rapid due diligence assessment up front puts external validation and depth of thinking into your plans. Announcing to the full organization the full "safe passage" process roadmap that shows all the launch events and quarterly checkpoints up front bolsters the plan with public commitment as well. In fact, prescheduling the dates of all major checkpoint meetings for the year really helps set a drumbeat that gets everyone's attention and won't be easily forgotten. Finally, setting, documenting, and communicating your personal Commitments to Action, which should include a commitment to lead the transformation process through the full cycle, will help seal your commitment and, therefore, the commitments of others.

Simple Closed-Loop Accountability

Having a tight vision and focus, absolute alignment of the organization, and high engagement of the full team are critical foundations for success. But these requirements are not enough. Without individuals throughout the organization staying committed to doing something different tomorrow than they were doing yesterday, the organization as a whole won't move forward.

Accountability in execution always starts at the top of the organization. Everyone needs a nudge now and then to keep focused and on track. A tight process can help keep you in the groove, but even that is not sufficient support for the leader. Serving as a nudge to the top leader can be a problematic role. For one thing, if your doctor keeps nagging you about lifestyle changes, it is really easy to just stop going to the doctor.

One CEO pointed out that following the transformation Launch Phase of the process, the need for continually driving the process forward was very tough and very much like going to regular checkups with the doctor. After the process was rolling and everyone was on track, he actually found it somewhat difficult to be the source of constant challenge and accountability. Indeed, it had actually crossed his mind several times to just let go of the process rather than feel the constant drumbeat on focus, follow-through, and accountability. The internal executive team members driving the process felt the heat as well. But being able to fulfill the role of a designated nudge is critical to keeping the focus and engagement of the organization high and the results moving forward.

Establish up front an unambiguous agreement that provides clear jurisdiction for your direct reports to call you out if your leadership of the transformation wanders. Between the integrity of the process and the open invitation to be nudged, your odds of following through go way up.

Without simple systems in place to track accountability, follow-through will elude the organization. However, these systems often evolve into administrative burdens that are so complex and time-consuming that managers simply don't use them. At a very basic level, the fact that numbers are tracked in a system doesn't provide any accountability. It is the closed-loop nature of returning to the objectives and goals repeatedly that matters most and that doesn't have to be all that fancy to work well.

To drive west from Newark Airport on Interstate 78 is to take a trip in a time machine. You pass from the industrial purposeful-ness of Newark to rolling hills splashed with dense stands of maples and birches, a world that seems almost colonial, with a ribbon of expressway surreally running through it. But as you exit the interstate deep into the Jersey suburbs, you first have to pass the sprawling, high-tech campus of a major telecom company. A bit farther on is a warehouse-like structure with an elaborate exoskeleton, reminiscent of the cheeky Pompidou Center in Paris. That's where a former cli-ent produces the gallium arsenide chips that are vital to cell phones, set-top boxes, and fiber-optics solutions. From the CEO's first day, he knew that the company needed the kind of business revolution he had helped generate at a much larger high-tech manufacturer earlier in his career as a general manager. His new company had launched as a highflier in the mid-1990s, but after it went public, several competi-tors turned up with slightly different processes for making chips. One of them had stolen his company's best customer and was working on second-generation technology that could make his firm obsolete. The new CEO knew he had to energize the senior executive team and leverage their capabilities to turn the company around.

The new CEO's agenda was first and foremost concerned about the experience of the Senior Leadership Team he had inherited. They were brilliant engineers, both creative and accomplished, but not strong on operational discipline. Instead of staying focused as a team and working efficiently to make timely decisions, they tended to spin unpredictably in their meetings, bringing more and different data to successive working sessions and constantly reopening old decisions rather than closing on new ones.

In the executive conference room a week into the CEO's term, eight members of senior management were gathering—and com-menting, a bit acidly, on the new gadget set up near the lectern. It was a "printing whiteboard," with a scrolling surface and equipment that prints out on paper. "I heard that [the new CEO] ordered it himself and it was pretty expensive," said one vice president. It had an imposing presence in the corner of the room but was soon forgotten as the CEO entered and the meeting started. He ran the session with force and skill, making it clear that the work they were about to undertake would be no picnic; new ways would have to be found to get things done. As the team ran through the big issues to be addressed, a few specific, short-term actions were suggested, each of which the CEO wrote on the whiteboard. In time, there were five items, ranging from getting direct feedback from key customers on where improvement was needed to exploring new technology processes that could completely change the industry. It was now late in the day. Energy was draining from the session. A few executives were stacking their papers and beginning to look at the clock. One floated a trial balloon: "Well, that was really a good session. There's clearly a lot for us to think about." Others inched toward the front of their chairs and looked at the CEO. But instead of signaling the end of the working session, he stood up and walked over to the printing whiteboard.

"You know," he said, "I've been in a few meetings here where great ideas are talked about, but nothing ever gets closed. Let's not let that happen with the things we've talked about today." Then he went through the five action items, assigning each one to a different member of the team and asking each executive to say what he could do with that issue in the two weeks before the team's next session. He wrote the assignments and commitments in a free-form grid on the whiteboard. The room buzzed a little as people realized, with some dismay, that this wasn't just feel-good talk about returning the company to its winning status. He clearly expected them to be accountable for important initial steps in the process—and in real, short-term time. "Good," he said. "Now it looks like we have a plan. Is everyone clear?" Agreeing quickly, they began to rise from their seats.

"Wait," the CEO said, "One more thing." He walked to the whiteboard, punched some buttons, and produced nine copies of the points and assignments that had been captured on the whiteboard. As each executive filed out, they received their copy of the action agenda, and he kept one for himself.

Two weeks later, when the CEO began the next session, he pulled out his copy of the whiteboard plan and began to ask for progress reports on each of the five action items. The message couldn't have been clearer: Discussion and dialogue were useful, but working sessions were intended to actually accomplish something. What is more, people were responsible for following through and would be called on it in follow-up sessions.

From then on, working sessions took on a new tone and rhythm. The team was far more focused and purposeful; each member was better prepared, knowing that real work was being done in the meetings and that records were being kept. Inevitably, the new discipline percolated through the whole organization as senior executives transmitted the new expectations down the line. In another example, the CEO of a heavy construction materials firm was driving a "good to great" transformation to elevate the company from $2 billion to $4 billion in annual revenues. He pointed out that building traction came down to

> two really nuts-and-bolts things. One is you need to create an ability to communicate from top to bottom. Then there are the little things...as far as writing things down and following back up with what we're going to do. We all know that the greatest trick to avoid any responsibility for your actions is to just be quiet and never say anything. If you are forced to get down on paper that this is what I'm going to do about this particular issue, then you take responsibility for it and go do it.

Promises Versus Declarations

What does accountability really mean? For some, it is a *promise*.

Do what you say you are going to do. That means setting sales goals, customer service goals, product launch dates, or other project delivery dates. Hit your goals and you keep your job; exceed your goals and you get some extra pay; but miss your goals too many times, and you are let go. This sounds pretty straightforward on the surface. However, the critical missing ingredient is an incentive for the individual performer to stretch beyond what seems imminently "doable." If the system under which your performance is judged is based on a firm promise, why would you ever sign up for a goal that you didn't already know you could reach? Under such a basis of accountability, it is in your best interest as a performer to set purposefully low goals or at least keep them in a range where no major risk or need for major breakthroughs or innovations is implied to win. In many real work situations, goals are things that simply need to be met, absolutely. For example, when we set a sales goal—a "promise"—it needs to be met at 100% or at least hit within a very narrow performance band. That is a world of accountability in which we normally operate. But the call for a shift in strategy, a major boost in growth or business performance, is not routine in its expectations. This is the domain of human activity, which is focused on getting from BIG ideas to BIG results.

An important distinction that is usually overlooked needs to be made and explicitly built in to accountability systems to unlock innovation and breakthrough thinking, which are the prerequisites to breakthrough success. In contrast to a promise, a commitment might be called for, about which it is not completely clear how to achieve, even if it is fully attainable. This might sound like heresy to you in the context of the normal performance management approaches used during steady-state conditions today. Think of this other dimension of accountability as making a *declaration—for a breakthrough*. For this discussion, consider a declaration as a commitment to shoot for an objective whose ultimate goal might at first be neither completely clear nor fully attainable. Although others have split much finer definitions of the words promise and declaration, to keep things simple and useable, consider a "promise" an absolute goal and "declaration" a statement of intent when the means to get there are unknown. The most notable declaration historically might be the one President Kennedy announced when he charged the National Aeronautics and Space Administration with putting a man on the moon before the close of the decade. To bring the declaration idea into focus, let's look at its dynamics in a real work situation.

Shoot for the Moon—Drive Innovation

One of the members of a West Coast team that accomplished a massive innovation effort understands the power unleashed by making declarations. On May 1, 1960, a U2, a U.S. spy plane, was shot down over the USSR. At the time, it was the only method for taking aerial photographs without the risk of being shot down, but that had just been proven wrong. Today, of course, we can all log on to Google Earth and have a look ourselves from the sky, but back then we were far from what we have today. With that event with the U2, President Eisenhower immediately accelerated a long-term project to develop satellite photography capabilities and demanded a working solution in just nine months. Of course, when the team of specialists, including Sam, were assembled, they had no idea if any of this was possible and certainly no idea of how to get it all done in nine months, but they took on the task anyway. They made a declaration for the "impossible."

A team of the best and brightest from multiple large corporations and government institutions was pulled together into what became project Corona. And it was definitely not a cold beer, feet in the sand type of beverage you might be thinking of today. This rapidly assembled group was told to do the impossible (at the time)—get a satellite up in space that was able to take pictures of the Earth with enough detail to be useful for reconnaissance and return the film to Earth—all of this without computers. As the team member describes it today, "We had 12 failures and missed the nine-month window." In the end, they had an explosion on the launch pad, many hurdles, and delivered two months late on the nine-month target. But they achieved the end goals. By statistical performance evaluation, you would say that they were 22% past the delivery date. It would be a failure in terms of meeting the promised date. But, of course, it was not a failure at all.

The Corona team generated technology breakthroughs that otherwise would have taken years, if not decades to be worked out and brought it from the labs into reality. After finally being declassified over 30 years later, the member received the prestigious Draper Award for the tremendous breakthroughs and innovations he contributed to that program. Obviously, the program was a success. If it had been handled in the traditional manner of "accountability" where the contractors had to promise a delivery date by signing a performance contract that would penalize late delivery and potentially set people up to be fired for not meeting the dates, do you think they would have shot for a nine-month delivery date—and delivered results in 11 months? Not a chance. That is the power of working in the realm of *declaration*. The team member's advice to large companies trying to drive innovation today, "You need to give people the freedom to innovate, let them set what seem like impossible goals for targeted breakthrough teams."

In a more recent example, the CEO of a chip company in Silicon Valley was reflecting on a declaration-type challenge he put forth to his team when he arrived. The challenge was to take the cycle time from order to ship from 17 weeks down to 3 weeks. Customers needed the cycle time to be faster. His people said it could not happen. They explained how this company was a special case compared to companies the CEO had worked at before. He explained to the team, "Let's just give it a try and see how far we get."

As they chipped away and built momentum, they got further than they thought they could. After several months of work, they had taken it from 17 weeks down to 3.5 weeks. Customers, of course, were delighted. The CEO chuckles, "Hey, they didn't really hit the goal of a three-week cycle time, but not bad, huh?"

During the process of shortening the cycle time, the team would gather for reviews with the CEO weekly. As they hit problems and delays, he jumped in with the team to solve the problems and come up with creative ideas to try. Some worked; some didn't. Working together under a clear declaration type of mandate to accomplish the "impossible"—as contrasted with a "promise" style—was a huge motivator for the team to strive for breakthrough performance.

This CEO understands the breakthrough in possibilities when you shift from managing promises to working declarations. He had played it out before, leading a company that manufactured microchips from below 70% product yields to over 90%, another so-called impossible goal by his team and peers. When asked how he came up with the idea for declaring for breakthroughs in this way, he explained:

> Way back, I was working for a Senior Leadership Team member who later became the CEO of his own semiconductor firm. When I joined his group, he told me the goal was to hit 100% product yields. Now that goal was for sure impossible. But he was relentless in the declaration. And in the end, he would measure us on how close we came and what ideas we could come up with for pursuing perfection. We always ended up with great yields and we were rewarded for that. It was uncomfortable at first seeing a goal written down that was such an obvious stretch, but it made us create some real breakthroughs.

The bottom line on accountability is that when leading a transformation and driving for innovations and performance breakthroughs, it is important to understand when you should be supporting the team to make *declarations* and when to be making *promises*. Make a clear distinction, or people will avoid taking risks with their plans and goals.

People wonder why the rate and magnitude of innovation is so low in companies. It is not because people have lost their creative edge or innovative thinking capabilities. It is that people are afraid to take the risks necessary to achieve breakthroughs. So you don't need wild off-sites to break out of the box; you need leaders to learn how to manage in a mode of declaration where sometimes projects will never achieve the goals set for them. People need to be able to fail, sometimes. Promise-laden accountability systems and approaches can inadvertently squash innovation. You need both promises and declarations; just be explicit about when you are in each mode.

Above and Below the Waterline

Clearly, there are some cases where you need to have an absolute commitment, a promise from your team, and others where you want the team to take risks. One of the good ways to determine when to apply declarations and when to apply promises is to categorize the type of issue you are facing. In some cases, there will be business-critical and time-critical issues that cannot slip. In those cases, ask for a promise. In other words, if you think about a boat on the water, if a hole was punched in the hull below the waterline, the boat will sink. These below-the-waterline issues need to be solved with promises. Set the goal with the team and then expect delivery. That's it. Shipment dates to customers, accuracy of financial statements, base revenues on core products—these often need to be treated as promises.

In contrast, when you are driving new growth, looking for new opportunities, looking to create competitive advantage by delivering breakthroughs in service or performance standards, you would be better served to make a declaration. Set the goal high, some might think it is impossible, and then work with the team to push it as far as possible. As an executive leading a new business-line initiative at one of the largest global retailers points out:

> Just the attempt at building a new business can generate huge breakthroughs that can be applied to our core business. This program is going to pay for itself just based on what we're going to learn and be able to apply across the company. We already know we'll end up with tools to better manage our field organization's efficiency and quality that can be used in the core business. If the new business itself plays out like we think it will, that will make it a home run.

If he had been told that the goal was to build a business that had $X in revenue by Y date and that his success or failure just rode on those two goals, he would have been forced to negotiate goals that were promises and work within the safety of known solutions and safe objectives. But with a declaration to launch a new, meaningful business for the company—one that had the potential for spinning off lots of innovations—his team has been able to play full out in a creative way to push the edges of innovation. They certainly need to deliver outputs, but there is no reason to limit them to known solutions; that's not the point, and that wouldn't drive innovation. As a result, they are playing above the waterline where if they fail, the boat won't sink.

Don't Get Overly Fixated on the Dashboard

Today there is an ability to control and manage almost every business process with software, and as a result, there is a huge amount of data available to use in setting up scorecards and dashboards. In general, the statement that "What gets measured gets done" is true.

However, if what gets measured turns into a complex system of data warehouses or massive Microsoft Excel spreadsheets with Pivot-Table reports or online tracking systems with thousands of different metrics to track, the realities of the business and of how everyone is performing can become hopelessly obscured.

If the complexity of the reports allows too many things to be measured and there is a long production lag, the metrics are useless. In driving breakthrough performance on a few major initiatives, what is needed is a simple scorecard of top-level metrics that externally validate if the stated strategies for executing the initiatives are working. Certainly, there is a good reason to have detailed internal metrics and scorecards to track tactical business processes across different functions.

Many things need to be targeted for continuous incremental improvements or monitoring. That's just good management. But when those same principles are applied to transformations and strategy execution, they break down. You need to select just a few important things that are targeted for quantum improvement in a short period of time. These things need to rise above the din of incremental change to focus everyone on the major drivers of quantum change. Otherwise, you will lose sight of what has the highest impact and leverage in achieving breakthrough results.

In addition, the scorecards can only tell you so much...and not always the full picture of reality. You've probably heard about one of the most famous but tragic incidents in aircraft disaster history, the crash of Eastern Airlines Flight 401 near Miami, Florida, on December 29, 1972. The pilot, copilot, and flight engineer had become fixated on a faulty landing gear light and had failed to realize that the autopilot had been switched off. Watching only their dashboard, they didn't see that the plane was headed toward the ground. The investigation concluded that the cause of the crash was pilot error. The distracted flight crew did not recognize the plane's slow descent, and the aircraft eventually struck the ground in the Everglades, killing 101 out of 176 passengers and crew. All the crew had to do was look out the windows and they would have seen their reality and been able to adjust. This is, of course, an extreme example, but the lesson learned is still clear today. Keep an eye on the dials, but don't lose sight of what is happening in the real world around you.

Ground Truth: The Real Results

There is a term in cartography and especially aerial and satellite photography that is called ground truth. *Ground truth* refers to information that is collected "on location" and "in reality" to validate what is being interpreted through high-level images or remote sensing systems. It calibrates what your systems are telling you to what is really going on. In other words, all the reporting systems in the world have flaws and are no substitute for true observations of reality—ground truth. More than just management by walking around in order to be seen as a leader of the people, it is a tool to keep an honest assessment of the front-line operations that are the reality that customers see.

The CEO of a several-hundred-million-dollar start-up that grew to over $14 billion in revenues explained his process for gaining ground truth. It was simple and effective. Each morning, he would come to the office and review results (sometimes actually starting the night before). He would take note of which areas were underperforming. However, he would not look at just the level of results right below him; he would look down into the details. That's why he sometimes started the night before. Then, when it came time to check on what was going wrong, he would not call in his direct report who owned the overall area. The CEO would call the lowest-level manager he could who owned the area that was having trouble. Needless to say, nobody was thrilled to get a call.

However, when the CEO called the manager, he would put him at ease and clearly state that he was just calling to help troubleshoot and see if there was anything he could do to help. He had an agreement with his direct reports and middle management that he would never tell somebody what to do, that was their job. On these calls, the CEO would simply question, challenge, and brainstorm with the manager of the underperforming area. Usually, they knew what to do and some had recommendations for more system-wide changes that were good ideas. If they had difficulty, he might help or suggest other peers or resources in the company to turn to as well. This process gave the CEO two things simultaneously. First, it was a clear message that the CEO cared about daily results and, therefore, so should everyone else. Second, it gave him a constant ground truth checkpoint on what was really happening in the organization.

A veteran executive of large companies and past CEO of a start-up shared a highlight of her career relating to ground truth. Unlike operating a start-up, executives in a large company can easily get far out of touch with what people are doing on the front lines to drive results on a daily basis. She points out that, "One of the most valuable things you can do as an executive is to find out what is really going on out in the field with customers." At one of the largest telecommunications companies in the world, she was serving as a VP of sales, and the organization was having a very tough time with order accuracy, which was negatively impacting customers on a daily basis. She tells of an amazingly simple, fast, and powerful approach the president of her group used to generate ground truth.

There had been an ongoing debate and finger-pointing about the problem of order accuracy within the staff management team. The president was fed up. His request to get the ground truth was simple. He requested that 25 sales support people, responsible for processing orders, keep a journal for a few weeks on everything they do on a daily basis. Then he wanted to gather the group together for a day, without all of the middle management, and go through their journals with them. That was it. She helped launch the effort and was invited to join the meeting. The sales support team members flew to corporate headquarters a few weeks after the project had been launched, and the president sat and listened carefully as every person read highlights from their journal and reported on what they had to go through every day. When they finished, the president looked around the table and declared, "Your jobs are impossible. What I don't get is how you can do them every day!" People laughed but explained their pride in the company and desire to help customers get what they needed.

This quick exercise pointed out exactly where the hot spots were that needed to be solved, and the president committed to making the changes quickly.

The president could have launched a task force of managers to look at the problem; he could have commissioned a months-long, time-and-motion and best-practices benchmarking study. Both of these would have taken more time and resulted in executive-level PowerPoint presentations for the president to review and approve.

Instead, in this case, he chose to go for the ground truth. And, as often is the case, the answers are not that tough to find and not that complex when viewed in the real world.

Finding ground truth is not just simply management by walking around or glad-handing the troops. It is about an authentic engagement between the leader and people who are closest to the customer in working-level jobs. Formalized field visits with the chief that are preplanned and scheduled are not views of reality. Those are artificial visits where everything has been shined and perfected for show. At one retailer, compliance to store audits was high, claims of progress to serve customers better were positive, and sales were improving. It all looked really good on the executives' balanced scorecards. However, a drive past the stores in person revealed sparsely populated parking lots compared to the competition, and employees on smoking breaks out in front of the stores. Entering the stores revealed a messy and less-than-welcoming atmosphere. The real progress was far behind what the reporting systems were showing. Not surprisingly, as executives in the company made more of a practice of casual drop-ins on the business, the initial pattern was confirmed—ground truth. Any system you put in place is prone to having blind spots or to being manipulated by those who can't and won't work to truly perform. That is the nature of monitoring systems. The only way to avoid running blind is to put ground truth reality checks in place for yourself and for leaders on your team to keep in touch.

Misguided Incentives

In addition to performance management, incentive systems need to be aligned as well. In a larger organization, it usually takes some time to plan how the performance management and incentive systems will be aligned to support the new Commitments to Action. Planning for this shift needs to begin as a parallel activity when the transformation effort is launched.

Often, there are conflicts between the strategic goals and the existing panoply of incentives. This inconsistency will always cause execution that is aligned with the priorities set by the incentive system and not with the new strategic goals. Natural self-interest is a primal driver. People follow the money. At times, leaders will allow incentives to be tied to an outdated success model while professing that people should "do the right thing" and follow the strategy. Even worse, some leaders make a distinction that "strategic" goals are those things that are tough to quantify and might not have a defined set of return-on-investment performance indicators. If your strategic initiatives can't be operationalized and tied directly to the financial success of the organization, don't take them on. They'll just become more money-losing executive pet projects.

The strategic initiatives that guide all of the organization's Commitments to Action need to be the most important and high-impact initiatives for the company. Being transformational in nature, they will need to be viewed as a restacking of priorities, which establishes a new baseline for daily operations. That doesn't mean you stop doing all of the normal daily tasks such as paying payroll, selling to new customers, and managing expense budgets. It just means that those need to be done in the right priority, alignment, and context within the new overall direction. If not, the initiatives become only ineffectual overlays to the way employees "really get things done around here!"

In short, when it comes to launching a fundamental transformation or new strategic initiative, virtually everyone's performance management objectives and incentive (bonus and salary) expectations need to be reset to achieve full alignment between the Transformation Initiatives and individuals' specific commitments. If the performance system also deals with values and behaviors (which it should), those need to be fully anchored in behavior change commitments as well. This alignment needs to start at the top of the organization with its executive leaders and then cascade in full alignment down through all managers and employees at all levels of the organization.

When challenging a business to generate breakthrough results, business as usual in all parts of the organization needs to be questioned. An executive vice president at a large corporation, who had also served as CEO of a successful start-up company, put it this way:

> In this corporate environment, we aren't able to reward excellence. It's a given that different people make very different levels of contributions. But what does it boil down to at the end of the year? The average raise percentage is set for the group at, say, 4%. The superstars get maybe 6% and everyone else gets 3% to 4%. At the start-up, we would pay people special bonuses and other compensation for making big contributions, and everyone was driving for the same wealth creation in the value of the stock. It was much more of a direct relationship. Why can't we put this flexibility and alignment in place inside a bigger company? We need to do that.

He is right; there is so much formality and complexity that managers have lost the ability to truly reward great performance and easily terminate nonperformers.

The strongest performance-oriented systems have two clear components. Performance-based pay is rooted primarily in external business performance indicators, not task accomplishment. You don't want a situation where everyone does well because they checked their task boxes while the real judges of performance, such as earnings growth, market share, and stock price, are falling. Any upside potential should be large for accomplishing the real-world gains—and this is the basis for compensation treatment.

On the other side, people ask, "How do we get people to do their daily tasks, then?" Simple. If people can't or won't do their daily tasks, they are let go. The opposite of good pay for a job well done should not be slightly lower pay for a poorly done job. However, that is the outcome of many systems today. The consequence of poor work over time should simply be to let the person go.

The Process Support Team

The requirement of a tight linkage between performance plans, incentive structures, and strategy necessitates a much more direct link between the various process disciplines within the company and those responsible for architecting the ACT-based process and leading the corporate transformation. It is a common mistake for this link to be made late in the process; instead, it needs to be established at the onset of the Launch Phase and kept in place throughout Execution.

One way to get this important support activity up and running is to formally develop a transformation Process Support Team that will ensure that all of the process disciplines (for example, Human Resources, Employee Communications, Performance Management, Training and Development, Strategic Planning, Organization Development, and so forth) are teamed together to provide direct and ongoing support in an aligned manner to the CEO and the SLT and ELT. The functional process leaders on this team must be among the first to reallocate their resources and align their plans to the ACT-based approach and major corporate Transformation Initiatives to support the line managers who are leading the effort.

Such a Process Support Team should be co-chaired by the Principal Process Architect of the corporate transformation and usually the company's Chief Human Resources Officer, to whom most of the functional process disciplines report. The Principal Process Architect is the ACT-based coach to the CEO and the SLT members, as well as to the Process Support Team. The Architect is usually from outside the organization and brings a wealth of CEO-led corporate transformation experience and know-how to the Team. It is the Process Architect's job to ensure that the process disciplines in the organization have the insights, tools, and templates to enable them to support the effort as it moves through the various phases.

The role of the senior staff officer occupying the Team's other Co-Champion role is to ensure that the functional process discipline leaders provide their support in a timely manner that is aligned with the ACT-based corporate transformation framework. This is often a challenging task because it inevitably means that many if not all of the process discipline leaders will have to give up previously important elements of their own game plan to be able to free up resources to reallocate to support needed from their function that is on the critical path of the corporate transformation. Indeed, some of these process leaders may initially have a difficult adjustment working in close collaboration with their staff peers. Again, it is the critical role of the internal Co-Champion to ensure that the various process function leaders quickly learn to work together in an aligned manner to be able to support the CEO and the Senior Leadership Team, and continue to do so on a just-in-time basis as the corporate transformation moves from each phase to the next. For all of these reasons, I've heard us say more than a few times in the kick-off meeting of a corporate transformation Process Support Team, "Buckle up; you're going to be on the front bumper of this transformation process, starting now!"

Performance Coaching

Frank and open conversations about performance are rare in companies today. These conversations end up confined to very formal and usually brief reviews of official documents that tie to raises, bonuses, career potential, and sometimes employment decisions.

To make matters worse, because performance isn't really discussed frequently enough, the conversations become superficial, and the final "scoring" of performance for an individual feels (and often is) too perfunctory and arbitrary. If the managers aren't consistently reviewing performance, they honestly won't have much depth to share as the basis of their evaluations. With all of the legal headaches and documentation requirements associated with performance management, managers tend to rate all of their people within a highly undifferentiated band. The great performers don't get rewarded enough, and the poor performers slide by, which breeds mediocrity.

This can happen not only at the individual level, but at the organizational level, where quarterly performance reviews on lines of business become missed opportunities to drive for excellence. As put by one seasoned Silicon Valley executive:

> There is way too much "happy talk" at the typical quarterly operations reviews. A company might be ahead of its own growth plan at 10%, for example, but if the market grew at 15%, it is actually losing ground. People spend too much time talking about all of the great things their organization did rather than focusing on what more could have been done. Everyone can always focus on improving, whether you are ahead or behind your numbers.

His perspective of needing to keep your performance in the context of the external market and maintaining a tough edge on always looking for improvement is what drives breakthrough performance.

Starting at the top, if the "happy talk" is allowed to permeate the quarterly checkpoints and performance reviews, there will be no compelling reason for any of the midlevel managers to engage their teams. They'll simply pass on the message: "Let's just keep going and everything is fine." People down the line feel relieved, and business-as-usual creeps in. If instead, each Quarterly Leadership Checkpoint is about recommitting to the overall speed and intent of the transformation, pushing progress further if milestones are achieved early, or course correcting where plans didn't unfold as anticipated, that will drive continual learning, commitment, and sustained performance improvement.

Tips for Building Corporate Transformation Traction

- Don't start anything unless you are fully committed to follow through.

- On the issues of accountability, know when to establish promises versus declarations.

- Create a transparent follow-through process that keeps everything transparent and under public scrutiny.

- End all meetings with clear accountabilities to get things done.

- Don't try to measure everything!

- Use scorecard reporting systems as one tool but don't fixate on dashboards and lose touch with reality.

- Set individual Commitments to Action (CTAs) throughout the organization.

- Align performance and incentive systems with CTAs up front.

- Stand up a transformation Process Support Team to engage and align the organization's process disciplines behind the corporate transformation game plan.

Endnotes

1. Alan Deutschman, "Change or Die," *Fast Company Magazine*, 2005, Vol. 95, p. 24.

10

Disruptive Innovation in Transformation

As we mentioned in the opening chapter, the frequency and severity of major industry and competitive disruptions are increasing. This chapter focuses on a new set of corporate transformation accelerators to enable leaders to both create and react more quickly to disruptive innovations in the market. These fast-paced changes in direction are referred to as corporate "pivots," a phrase borrowed from start-ups who begin down one strategic path that does not play out and have to find an entirely new strategy and value proposition to continue in business.

Beyond the speed to breakthrough results found through the well-designed simplicity and compression of ACT, we have also identified new accelerators and capabilities that enhance an organization's ability to compete in the age of disruptive innovation. What is fueling the level of disruptive innovation in our marketplaces? First, technology has won. A decade or so ago, it was high-tech companies that had to cope with dramatically compressed cycle times. Miss just one beat, and you were likely eclipsed by an innovative rival or new competitor with a disruptive business model, product, or solution. Now, almost every company is becoming a tech company. All types of products and services have become deeply infused with sensors, intelligence, and controls that put compressed technology cycles at the heart of the value proposition. Entirely new value is being generated by building smart-connected platforms on top of traditional businesses like car services, hotel booking, entertainment services, factory automation, building management, healthcare, and others. This makes the traditional products and services operate in a short high-tech innovation cycle.

Second, the ability for small companies to scale quickly with new business models has become apparent as one traditional industry after another is falling under the accelerating wheels of heretofore unknown or at least unrecognized competitors. Many organizations have become so focused on their traditional adversaries and global encroachers that they are being leap-frogged by new entrants from left field. Once-secure players in retail, travel, publishing, and photography are being laid low by disruptive competition and innovation, and the waves are coming closer and closer together. Even as we write this, disruptive "fintech" models are hammering away at the world-class American banking industry. Virtual banks without bricks and mortar have been gaining traction, and the New York Stock Exchange recently announced a strategic investment in a bitcoin wallet provider. As the CEO of one of America's leading banks recently wrote in his most recent letter to shareholders, "There are hundreds of start-ups with a lot of brains and money working on various alternatives to traditional banking." As the head of a firm that researches private companies recently cautioned, "Right now we're in the awareness phase. Companies that fail to act risk 'death by a thousand cuts.'"[1]

As much as industries and companies are being disrupted and, hence, must transform, the same disruptive technologies and approaches to business can be applied to how transformations are launched and implemented. These new capabilities include leveraging purpose as a burning ambition and applying design-centered principles to generate more customer-centric innovative strategies at the front end of a transformation. To effectively sustain the engagement of large teams dispersed across the globe, the capabilities of applying social media engagement and wisdom-of-the-crowd thinking are driving greater collaboration, engagement, alignment, and commitment in transformation across organizations at all levels. Finally the concept of transformation being only a set of major multiyear, capital-intensive programs that will eventually show benefit down the road has given way to a need for running transformation as an agile business innovation cycle with immediate sprints to value, with agile pod-team structures focused on creating customer value and impact as quickly as possible.

Purpose-Infused Transformation: The Three I's

Purpose has become a central concept in how companies define the essence of why they exist. It is inherently rooted in the concept that successful businesses exist to make the lives of their customers better and have a reason for being and way of being in the world that is needed and appreciated. It should be no surprise that purposeful companies have more loyal customers, attract better talent, have leading market share, and enjoy premium value positions in the market. For similar reasons associated with driving market success, Purpose has emerged as a powerful accelerator for driving corporate transformation.

As you launch a corporate transformation, you know that getting the team to work differently, behave differently, and relate to each other and customers differently will not be easy. Some people think of this activity as the field of change management. But in reality, change is not something to be "managed," it is something to be "unleashed" in *every* person in the organization.

As a starting point, you need to first think about shifting your leadership mindset. If you believe that people hate change and that it is your job to change them, they will hate it. If you believe that people thrive on change and that your job is to unleash it, you will tap into a limitless source of ingenuity, energy, and drive that will allow you to consistently take your big ideas into big results. To bring this mindset to action, apply the three I's of purpose-infused transformation.

Together, they can help you shift your approach to be more effective in achieving transformational results.

Inspire: The basic low-bar standard for explaining a transformation to your team should be nothing short of having them become inspired. Every person needs to become self-motivated and creatively engaged. For example, a "case for change" PowerPoint that explains how higher customer satisfaction scores of various kinds will increase market share for the company may be factual, but not inspiring. And burning platforms intended to provide tough love messages of "change or else..." may drive some fear-based action, but not inspiration. This factual information, even the brutal facts, has an important role to play in catalyzing understanding about the need to transform, but these facts always come up short as motivators.

Purpose is built around understanding "why" an organization exists and how it benefits others. A strong Purpose changes the focus—toward doing things for customers, coworkers, and others to make their lives better. At Starbucks, the global coffee maker, the Purpose is, "To inspire and nurture the human spirit—one person, one cup and one neighborhood at a time." When sharpening your Transformation Arrow, centering the strategy, brand, culture, and values on Purpose establishes a greater sense of shared meaning. Throughout the organization. It shifts the focus to a shared "burning ambition" to achieve something as a team that will benefit others and each other, that becomes inspiration.

Internalize: When you're a leader, when driving transformation, there is a rule that "you can't want it more than your team." If you first inspire, people will individually understand and want to achieve the transformation themselves. Each person should be invited to think deeply about how he or she can individually change behavior, actions, decisions, work patterns, and interactions with others to achieve success. The question becomes, "How can I individually become the transformation that we want to achieve together?" This happens not just by handing people a detailed training book on how to do their jobs differently or a new customer service script. The best way we have found to accomplish this is through the rollout of a *Rapid, High-engagement, All-employee Cascade*, which creates a setting in which employees can explore the company's Purpose, how that drives the need to transform and then engages employees in deciding how to make that happen as a team and for themselves.

Impact: For follow-through in a transformation, if all that happens is to print T-shirts and posters and logo coffee mugs about the program and publish a quarterly red-yellow-green dashboard report, all is lost. With Purpose, we talk about impact being measured by observable positive impact on others, not achieving milestones or work tasks. Today there are a number of ways to measure impact that can complement the standard performance metrics, which may include social media scanning of customer posts, job boards, or industry-focused sites. It could also include real-time monitoring of the customer experience or watching competitors try to copy your moves. Even at a personal level, a customer service representative could have the goal to have the most customers every day say, "Wow, you just made my day!" Every time that happens it is a motivator to do more, and it has a visible impact that reinforces the new behaviors.

These are not standard "initiative key performance indicators," but instead, they are powerful ways to shift from simply achieving tasks to generating breakthrough results. Reinforcement, application, and dedication to the transformation results every day and in every interaction are what will ultimately translate into impact.

Design-Centered Strategic Thinking

Over the last ten years there has been a strong and steady movement toward a new way of strategic thinking, one that is design-centered at its core. Based on the pace and level of disruption in the marketplace today, corporate strategy has moved from an exercise in planning and predicting areas for long-term business growth and improvement to a focus on constantly innovating, designing, and defining entirely new ways to provide customers with value in a real-time flow.

A design-centered way of thinking about strategy challenges the classic view of corporate strategy as a statement of what the company is good at (core competencies) and owns (assets) into more of a view of what the company is good for (its purpose in the world). When focusing on what a company is good for in the world, the perspective changes from internal planning to a concentration on the way a company's products and services make the lives of customers, employees, and stakeholders better.

A design-centered strategy development team looks different than a classic team of corporate strategy MBAs. A central premise in design is to start by defining a challenge to be solved by looking at the needs and value to a person or group of people. This perspective can be built by intentionally mixing skills, educational backgrounds, and mindsets across your strategy team. This would include members with classic MBA or business backgrounds, those with design degrees, and those with a mix of human-centered degrees such as anthropology and sociology. The work the team conducts focuses on deeply understanding the needs of customers as individuals and developing new ways to meet those needs better and more completely than competitive alternatives. One way to think about the work is to develop strategies that simultaneously *disrupt* old models of business and *delight* customers in new ways. If the strategy does not accomplish these two objectives, it is not yet sound. This strategic pair of criteria go further to stretch the imagination of what is possible in the strategic plans than just targeting a reasonable revenue growth stretch goal.

The design-centered approach focuses on optimizing how much better the lives of customers (consumer or business) could be made with a new solution to their needs. If the solution is highly valuable to customers and there is a broad-based gap in serving their needs, there will be willingness to spend. The market size can be validated, and so in the end it will still generate revenue growth as an outcome of the strategy. This new approach sits in contrast to more traditional views of developing strategy based on research of existing markets, looking for those that are growing and are large, and then determining how to gain market share with new products or services.

As an example, a retail convenience store operator was planning to update store designs to turn around a trend of flattening sales. Using a design-centered strategic approach, they first moved to identify which customers were coming into the store after stopping to fill up their cars with gas and at what time of day they were making the stop. Based on the initial research, it became clear that women and Millennial customers were stopping for gas but not entering the c-store. The design question asked, "What is our experience not delivering that would make the life of the women and Millennial customers better if we had a different offering?" The answers were tough to hear. They ranged from the name and exterior of the store to the food displays and the selection of products themselves. In essence, just about everything about the c-stores was wrong for these customers.

The executive team realized that the brand, store design, food vendors, merchandising displays, and branding of the store would all have to change to serve the needs of these currently excluded people. Believing in design-centered strategic thinking, the company built a view of the ideal experience that included women and Millennials and conceptualized an entirely new store format. When finished, they developed pilot stores to test their new design. Immediately, they began generating over double the revenue from the new store formats. The new experience was fully designed for a targeted set of people who in the past were not customers of the c-store. Almost none of the old concept or assets were maintained in the new model. The company had pivoted to the previously unserved market needs, designed a great experience, and achieved the new growth they were seeking. This approach stands in contrast to an inside-out view of taking the old model and customers as a given and then working to optimize and improve incrementally the operating cost, customer services, or merchandise, as shown in Table 10.1.

Table 10.1 Classic Versus Design-Centered Strategic Thinking

	Classic Strategy	Design-Centered Strategy
Strategy Team Skills	Business	Business, design, anthropology, sociology
Strategic Opportunity	Market size and growth	Unmet or underserved customer needs
Prioritization of Initiatives	Return on investment and ease of implementation	Impact on customer value and ability to execute
Sustainable Competitive Advantage Based on	Experience curve, assets, intellectual property	Depth of customer understanding and connection, pace of innovation, and superior customer experience

It has become much more common now to see design thinking and skill sets embedded and blended with traditional corporate strategy teams. As an example, one of the top venture capital firms in Silicon Valley recently hired the former president of a top global design school to help bring design thinking as a growth lever to their portfolio companies, underscoring the importance design has taken in driving business innovation and growth.

When preparing your team to confront reality and conduct the outside-in look at the business, consider building a design-centered team with a mix of skills and a design-centered strategy development process.

Enterprise Social Media and Wisdom-of-the-Crowd

Another of the disruptive forces in business has been the growth and power of social media. And as powerful of a tool for communications, engagement, sharing, and collaborating social media has become in our personal lives, it is just beginning to be exploited as a driver in corporate transformations.

Two of the most critical determinants of success in transformations are how well the total organization is engaged in the process and how invested people are in shaping the actual Transformation Initiatives themselves.

In the past, many executive leaders have relied on internal communications tools that were primarily focused on pushing messages out from headquarters to the broader organization, sometimes accompanied by sporadic employee surveys or town hall meetings, which allowed for employee input, feedback, and ideas. But with the speed of change today, these tools lag the immediacy required to succeed with large-scale transformations and do not scale well across globally distributed teams.

To provide an example, a global leader in mobile communications was working through a transformation of its technology organization. The firm's transformation leaders saw before them a big challenge of driving transformation through an organization that was highly geographically dispersed and yet collectively held deep expertise that could be useful in shaping the Transformation Initiatives at all levels of the organization. Recent efforts to transform the big company turned into a series of short-term bursts of focus and attention that would fizzle out in less than a single performance year. Leaders were unable to maintain that level of collaboration, communications, engagement, commitment, and drive to build a sustained effort on execution. The need to transform continued to build in importance as the pace of market disruption and innovation increased in the market. Continued unabated, one of the answers to sustaining the next transformation attempt, the organization developed an ACT-based process to guide the transformation and in parallel designed an enterprise social media–based engagement platform that leveraged corporate versions of blogging, crowd-source idea generation, and user-generated content.

The core of the platform was a blog site, available only to employees, which became the primary way for all employees to find information, stay up to date, provide input and ideas, and look for ways to engage in the process. The site launched with a series of video blog posts from the top executive team. These were short video clips intended for you to feel like you walked into an executive's office, and there he or she described the focus of the transformation directly to you. Interestingly, these videos became the highest-ranking content in the entire platform over time. Employees felt that they were hearing the truth about transformation straight from the organization's leaders. The videos were bringing a level of personal connection to every employee on the global team. And as one staff member pointed out to us, in the past only the people who were in place at the launch of a new corporate Transformation Initiative would understand the reasoning behind it. Now, every new employee was directed to watch the videos to both "get to know" a bit about the executive team and to also learn what the transformation was all about. In addition, due to the popularity, it became almost impossible for those same executives to move away from the commitments they made to the organization to follow through on the transformation; so that their commitment and focus on follow-through remained extremely high. This enterprise social media platform gave ongoing life to the model of a high-engagement, all-employee cascade, and quarterly checkpoints. The engagement in transformation was active every day, all the time. Another form of leveraging the motivation created by making individual, in this case leaders', Commitments to Action publicly transparent.

Beyond the Launch Phase, the platform was expanded to include subpages dedicated to each Transformation Initiative. The leaders of each Transformation Initiative were required to have their team post meeting notes, status updates, and requests for input and ideas in their areas. This allowed all employees to track progress and stay up to date, as deep into the information they wanted and also when they had the time to dive into the content. It was impossible for employees to feel out of connection due to communications gaps as all of the information was immediately accessible, up to date, yet also inclusive of a growing history of each initiative area.

In addition to the blogging and video platforms, the transformation leadership team set up innovation jam sessions where both in real time as well as for designated periods of time, specific challenges with the transformation would be raised and any employee could participate in the process of brainstorming and sharing ideas. These open jams became a way for every employee with motivation and interest to work with executives in developing answers to some of the toughest challenges confronting the transformation. This approach reinforced the idea of open engagement, built high engagement and involvement, and provided the executive with fresh and very practical ideas on demand.

As the content gained more history and depth, there were some unexpected benefits to the new level and style of communications and engagement. Key statistics from the platform began to reveal lapses in follow-through by certain teams. When the number of new posts from the team fell off and blog posts became less frequent, the transformation support team knew it was time to step in to help revive not just the communications, but the entire initiative. It turned out that the social media activity related to a Transformation Initiative was a real-time indicator of the level of activity of the team and engagement by the organization. There was no need to wait for a quarterly update or an employee engagement survey to notice that activity around a specific initiative was lagging; the feedback was immediate. This allowed much faster response to leaders who were stuck with their initiative and kept accountability to execute high, making it a powerful way to scale, speed, and sustain employee engagement and commitment beyond the ACT-based cascades and quarterly checkpoints.

We are just on the front edge of discovering the full impacts of enterprise social media on how we share ideas, engage people, collaborate, and build accountability in real time. We now suggest that a robust development of a social media platform be built to support any corporate transformation game plan. And as new models of communication and idea generation are developed, try applying them to project teams driving the Transformation Initiatives, which are struggling down in the organization to stay focused and consistent in their implementation efforts. There will never be a substitute for face-to-face communications as well as the initial and ongoing engagement and commitment setting of the ACT-based, *Rapid, High-engagement, All-employee Cascade* and quarterly mini-cascades in transformation work—but social media interventions have the potential power to place engagement and consistent implementation on a real-time and, indeed, virtual basis.

Agile Business Innovation

The fourth transformation accelerator we have discovered is the application of agile principles to the way in which departmental and cross-functional project teams are developed and run to drive Transformation Initiatives down in an organization. A common way to build such teams, in the good name of alignment and engagement, is to name a team leader and provide them with a cross-section of team members representing each stakeholder group in the company. These can easily become 20- to 30-member teams made up of those who are each perhaps 5%–10% time-allocated to the initiative. This feels like a huge resource commitment of talent, but with such a small commitment of each member's time at work, there is abundant opportunity for distraction and loss of focus and ultimately hit-or-miss implementation.

Borrowing from the technology practices of agile software development, we have been working with clients to build project teams that are small in size, high in time commitment, and time-boxed to deliver tangible outcome value in short sprints. To make decisions and drive rapid progress with an initiative, we have found that teams of five to seven deep experts, who are each dedicating 80% or more of their time to work on the initiative, to be ideal. Some people call this the two pizza rule, meaning that if you can't feed your hard-working team with two pizzas, then the team is too big. Regardless of the reasoning, the smaller and more dedicated project teams often have a lower staffing cost than the larger teams and can work in much more compressed time frames. In addition, the level of trust built between team members becomes very strong, leading to greater breakthroughs over time.

In addition to the structure of the teams, another important concept in driving an agile business approach is to focus on outcome value of the team's work. In agile software development, this is referred to as minimum viable product or focusing on delivering the most value to the end customer as possible in the shortest amount of time. With the agile approach, teams are directed to identify a portfolio of benefits that their team can deliver and design their work plans and milestones to focus on driving customer impact and value. This emphasis results in work plans that accelerate beyond planning and into having an impact on employees and customers and turn the traditional longer-term planning exercises into a cycle of taking action, testing the impact, and then improving for the next cycle.

There are some simple principles you can follow to establish your project teams to drive transformation initiatives down in your organization using key agile business concepts:

- Set up a small dedicated team of five to seven people, each of whom is allocated 80% or more to do the team's core work.
- Require that the dedicated core team actively engages the larger cross-functional perspectives early, efficiently, and regularly, perhaps leveraging the social media and wisdom-of-the-crowd platform you develop.

- Develop work plans and milestones that are based on delivering outcome value at each step, in 30- to 90-day sprints.

- Refrain from building complex and long-term plans; instead, bias the teams toward executing against a constantly evolving portfolio of activities that are improved through trying and refining.

There is much more to be said about running agile teams, but in the spirit of agility, take these initial ideas and design your project teams in support of your next transformation attempt around these principles.

Especially when transformations are targeted at responding to a disruptive innovation threat or as a preemptive move, the level and speed of change are amplified greatly as compared to more traditional operational or incremental change efforts. These keys of starting with design-centered strategic thinking to spark innovative strategies, leveraging enterprise social media more virtually and scale engagement, and running in an agile business innovation approach bring new facets to how you can run a transformation effort at top speed with real-time engagement. These approaches are equally valuable and can be applied to all types and levels of transformations as well, not just high-speed pivots. And in fact these accelerators, like the ACT foundations, should become a part of the way leaders run their businesses every day.

Tips for Leveraging Disruptive Transformation Methodologies

- Develop a burning ambition for the entire organization that is rooted in the core purpose of the enterprise.

- Build new capabilities in design-thinking into your innovation and strategic planning.

- Leverage cross-disciplined and diverse mindsets to solve problems in new ways, crossing business, design and technology.

- Employ enterprise social media and collaboration tools to leverage the engagement of globally dispersed teams.

- Tap into the wisdom-of-the-crowd.

- Shift the business processes and culture to embrace working with agility and speed to ensure rapid transformation toward becoming a proactive disruptor.

Endnotes

1. "Look Out, Big Banks: Here Comes 'Fintech,'" *USA Today*, May 18, 2015, p.1B

11

Are You Up to the Challenge?

The best way to end any working session is to launch into the work of the next phase before the meeting breaks up. Similarly, the best way for you to end the book is by launching your next phase of leading transformative, breakthrough performance in your organization. But before you do, you have to do a personal gut check. Are you prepared to make a BIG personal commitment to see things through? Are you ready to convert your BIG ideas into BIG results?

White-Hot Commitment of the Leader

Every seasoned executive in the world who drives breakthrough performance always shares one central observation about being a successful leader—that you have to have an unwavering commitment to seeing things through. Any sense of hesitation, lack of confidence, or quick blink, especially during the Execution Phase will result in a massive loss of energy across the organization. You must be willing to personally serve as both the catalyst to get things started and the energy core to keep it going. Not everyone is up for the challenge.

One veteran who had been CEO of several *Fortune 500* public companies has led transformations for growth, for adaptation to massive regulatory shifts, and even for the survival of a bankrupt corporation. One of the main causes of success or failure is what he calls the "white-hot commitment of the leader." This is a deep, personal commitment to fundamental improvement that the leader needs to make before stepping up front to lead others through a corporate transformation effort. If you are not willing to take personal risks, you won't be able to lead your organization from BIG ideas to BIG results. Hedging bets leads at best to incremental change and, more likely, to failure. As the CEO points out, "It goes beyond the bounds of your current job and into the core of who you are and what you believe."

To take this big step as a leader, you also need strong commitment from those to whom you directly report. If you are the CEO, you need the Board behind your efforts. If you are a division president, you need the CEO behind you. You might have to step up initially to make a stronger commitment than you are able to get from above, but to do so successfully, you need at least the support to make the tough decisions, personnel changes, and investments required for success. In fact, all levels of managers will need an appropriate level of latitude to operate and make decisions as well. Realistically, you won't even recognize half of what needs to get done or approved until you actually Launch your corporate transformation and begin the process of learning from execution. Just take care to keep people above you in the learning loop as you move forward.

But be especially cautious about responding affirmatively to a request from above to lead a transformation when you have been given no latitude. If the gap between expectations and latitude is too wide for you to comfortably and effectively operate, consider doing something else. Otherwise, you'll find yourself in a no-win situation, and your talents might be better leveraged working for a leader who will both expect great things and support you in taking the risks to achieve them.

Sometimes, the initial idea of launching a transformation does not originate at the top. When an executive vice president and CFO strongly felt a major transformation opportunity at his heavy construction materials company was required, he was sensitive to the need for support from above. He worked to secure the alignment and commitment from above that he knew would be necessary. Quickly, after being introduced to the corporate transformation game plan, the CEO became committed and in the lead. Following the successful transformation of the company, which as a result doubled its market capitalization in just two years, the CFO reflected that the CEO "constantly amazed me that his commitment was stronger than mine, and that enabled me not to worry about continuing to have a commitment. That makes it work."

Change the People, or Change the People

Often during transformations, the shift in requirements for personal leadership, competencies, and commitment will drive the need to change out team members. How this is done or not done on its own can undermine an otherwise great transformation effort. The most common challenge is when top leaders challenge their teams to behave on the job in new ways, live a new culture, and adopt a high-engagement approach to leading their part of the transformation. Many times, after those expectations are set, various senior leaders can't or won't make the changes in themselves. Often, they can remain out of alignment for quite a long period of time, during which they cast a pall over those in each level below them. If they are permitted to persist in this state of misalignment, the damage to the credibility of the leader and his or her transformation effort will be enormous.

Reflecting back on the defining moment in his transformation several years later, one of the successful high-tech CEOs with whom we have worked expressed regret at not having acted more quickly on the problem of executive nonalignment:

> We had one or two executives who I knew from the get-go were not the right people, and there were two or three others who over time basically came to me and said, "What the process expects of us is too hard." So part of the defining moment for me was determining who's going to stay on the team and

who's going to go. To me, that is the biggest thing. Of the people who deselected themselves, I would say that at least half of them I had an inkling in the bottom of my heart that I had to change those guys. But you hesitate. Don't hesitate. Give yourself 90 days in total to do all the assessments, evaluations, getting to know people, and getting to know their strengths and weaknesses and what they've contributed. But after 90 days, make those changes. Don't wait two years for some of them to quit on you. I would be more aggressive on that front.

One of the reasons to use the ACT-based *Rapid, High-engagement, All-employee Cascade* process is to create a clear shaft of expectations from top to bottom in the organization that enables misaligned behaviors to be spotted and dealt with before they pollute the whole effort. Also the speed of the process helps to smoke out the pretenders and footdraggers right away. However, when the resisters surface or declare themselves, all eyes immediately focus on how the top leader will react. If nothing is done, the whole thing becomes a farce. In contrast, when decisive action is taken either to demand alignment or to remove the head fakers, a reverberation is sent through the organization that reinforces the transformation. This can be most challenging when long-term colleagues and friendships exist between the leader and the wayward manager.

But there is a very positive side to this situation as well. According to the CEO and COO of a national retailer, one of the most surprisingly beneficial aspects of running through the high-engagement cascade process was seeing fantastic talent that otherwise was "below the radar" of the senior team. At the initial Confronting Reality and later during the Cascade sessions with the top 300 or so leaders, they admitted that people they had otherwise pigeonholed or didn't notice before actually stepped up and surprised them in terms of the quality of leadership, strategic thinking, and operational savvy. You don't normally get to see these people, and often they get buried under weaker bosses who don't give them the opportunity to be exposed to the senior leadership team. When you create an opportunity for these people to show up, you find new talent in the organization that you can enlist in driving the transformation forward. These people can become the replacement leaders for those who can't or won't make the necessary changes.

The takeaway is that nonaligned personnel changes also have to happen quickly. The damage done by a misaligned leader transcends the impact on the entire effort to shift the business by revealing that the overall leader is unable to make tough but obviously necessary decisions. As a result, people conclude, "Why should I change at my level if they won't take care of business at the top?"

When one of our clients, who was president of the European Division, became CEO of the whole company, he faced the need to very quickly turn around the company's performance. He knew that he needed leaders who could both drive stronger business performance and model the desired culture. He repeatedly encouraged two of his senior executives, who were driving good business results, to align their behaviors with the agreed-upon values. When it was clear they had no intention of following the new values, he fired both of them and announced to the entire organization why he did so. His decisive actions taken early in the post–Launch Phase of the corporate transformation sent a shot across the bows of other nonaligned senior executives who likewise were casting negative shadows over thousands of employees below them. The CEO followed and often communicated the idea that in order to generate breakthroughs, "You need to change the people, or change the people." Not surprisingly, a year later the company had achieved dramatic improvements across all three of its transformation initiatives.

Jack Welch, who fundamentally transformed General Electric during his long tenure as CEO, was perhaps the first to outline this essential requirement of successful transformation leaders. His basic message was that for transformations to be successful, they must be borne by leaders who can both drive breakthrough results *and* lead the right way. The two key dimensions of leadership are both required. Jack extended this insight by observing that the most dangerous leaders—the ones who can ultimately bring down a transformation—are those who drive up their results but do it through a leadership style that is not in alignment with the desired new company culture and values. The real danger is that because for a time they can deliver strong, short-term results, they can be easily ignored until the way they lead causes real damage.

Indeed, this was the situation our CEO had on his hands. The two leaders in question were achieving results, but clearly not modeling the new culture. Rather than let them undermine the entire transformation process, he let them go, despite their results. At that point, the message was clear. Get in alignment or be prepared to pass the mantel of leadership to someone else. For those who thought their results would always protect them, this came as a thunderclap. To the rest of the executives left standing, it showed that he was serious and that it was time to seriously get on board. A second problem is the situation in which people are producing mediocre "B" or "C" level results, but are extremely supportive of the new culture. It can be tough to know how to handle this group as well. They are well-meaning and hugely optimistic but just don't come through with the hard business results. They are all heart but have the wrong skills for the job. These people must also be dealt with quickly, either moving them to jobs where they can be effective in driving results or releasing them if they are not a fit for what is needed.

Another seasoned CEO of large and small technology companies pointed out to us that, "The first goal is to get the 'A' players behind the effort. Then, quickly address those who are behind the transformation but not generating results. If too many 'B' and 'C' players who are enthusiastic to change the culture but aren't driving results line up first, it can be a misleading signal to the 'A' players that the transformation isn't about results and they won't join the effort. And this challenge needs to play out at multiple levels of the organization."

The key here is that you need to develop a core team of "A" players who can both drive results and lead the right way. That is a primary and central task of a great transformational leader.

You Don't Have All the Answers (And Nobody Expects You To)

The CEO and COO of a big box office supply company were about to launch their transformation effort to the full organization after having worked through confronting reality, sharpening the strategy, and aligning the Senior Leadership Team. The team clearly had ownership and accountability but still seemed hesitant to move forward. The COO, a no-nonsense business leader, gathered his team and broke the ice by saying, "I think people aren't comfortable that we're really ready to spring this on everybody quite yet." There were lots of nodding heads and a few knowing glances cast about looking for approval. He went on, "Today, we need to get everybody on the same page and ready to go before we kick this off next week." He signaled clearly that he wasn't bugging out, just trying to ease the team's anxiety. Now it became a matter of figuring out how to make people more comfortable.

Each leader was going to be charged with spurring dialogue at a tablework group at the upcoming cascade working session. They would be there to provide clarity when needed—but above all, they were *not* to dominate the conversation. The real sticking point was expressed by a nervous vice president of operations who said it quite plainly: "Well, I don't think we have much to roll out—there's not enough here. I won't stand up in front of everyone and say we don't really have a complete plan yet. It will make us look like we don't know what we're doing. I won't do it."

So there it was, the real reason people were hesitant to move forward.

A lot of leaders believe their job is to have all the answers and be able to give specific orders to their teams. But that's not what people necessarily expect, need, or want. Sure, they want leaders to have a sense of vision, direction, boundary conditions, and measures of success, but they don't want to be told exactly what to do. They want to own their jobs and take pride in their performance, to contribute something, to be valued for their knowledge. Telling everyone what to do squelches job ownership and individual drive, two great assets that every workforce should have.

The CEO and COO reminded the executive team that they together had already gone through such a shift when they had opened up the dialogue about the corporate strategy to the full executive team just a few weeks earlier. They shared that they had personally felt the same dynamic as they opened up themselves to the executive team more for ideas for strategy development rather than telling everyone their answers. As the executive team members reflected on how being included in the dialogue felt and had benefited them, they began to make the connection about why they should be leading their teams in a similar fashion. The CEO and COO had approached their team with challenges and overall direction but not all of the answers, which is exactly what had motivated the executives to put innovative ideas on the table and address long-standing problems that had been written off as "givens" in the business.

A few days later, the operations VP engaged his full management team. He shared his views on the Transformation Initiatives, goals, and metrics. A lively dialogue unfolded during the tablework sessions that followed. At the end of the meeting, the VP walked away with some great input to make his plans, making them sharper and more "implementable" in the field. His managers were now engaged; they had ownership over the Transformation Initiatives and were volunteering to help fine-tune them before cascading them out through all the regions and stores.

For some, it is quite difficult to get over the idea that the boss needs to have all of the answers. One manager, who later became an executive with a 4,000-person round-the-clock global operation, pointed out the key differences very clearly. At one point in his career, he and a coworker held identical jobs. Both were "on call" as managers all of the time. Nights, weekends, holidays—the phone would ring. The coworker had a more autocratic style, and everything had to come through him, and when it did, he would immediately snap into action, get the right people on the phone, and drive for quick decisions. The other executive would instead ask the caller the simple question, "Do you know what needs to be done?" Most always, the caller would have an answer and usually it was right on point. The executive would close by saying, "Just go ahead and do what you need to do, and drop me a note on my desk on any documentation that I need to see when I get back." As the executive pointed out, his job got easier over time, and he really did believe that his people knew what to do in their specific areas of responsibility. The autocratic coworker was left to field more and more calls where everything came through him and people wouldn't dare to think for themselves.

Get Real

At the root of the ability to serve as a transformational leader is how grounded you are, how authentic you are, how "real" you are. For instance, a leader of a district overseeing two of California's community colleges has been widely recognized for her work as a transformational leader in her field. She puts this ability in very clear terms as a personal challenge:

> To transform an organization, you need to be willing to transform yourself. I feel the most powerful as a leader when I have alignment of the strength in my heart and openness in my thinking in my head. Too often, we try to just think our way through transformations, with everything in the head.

You need a balance among the depth, intuition, openness, and listening that comes from strength within your heart and body as well as the thinking around goals, deliverables, and metrics that happens in your head.

Your ability to connect deeply with your team correlates directly with the ability to build the trust and inspiration necessary for people to take the risks required to move into execution of the transformation. People know when you are playing full-out in an authentic way. And they know when you're holding something back, calculating your moves, and manipulating the situation. You can sense the authenticity of your moves from observing the passion and commitment of all of the people around you. Say what's in your heart, keep it simple, act in a way that is true to who you are, and you'll show up as a *real* leader. You serve in this way as a leader, and you'll put your transformation in motion.

Go for It!

The business world is constantly moving faster, and the "new normal" has become a constant state of disruptive change, or transformation. Any winning formula today is copied, improved, or undermined too quickly to get stuck in one business model.

Many of the systems, approaches, and management programs that have been used for years are so over engineered in how they get deployed that they are rejected by organizations now sick of the program-of-the-month cycle. Moreover, if actually implemented, they create Gridlock as one program is layered on another in a patchwork of Band-Aids that actually sets up conflicting priorities and stretches resources too thinly to matter.

Now that you've finished reading this book, let's be clear that nobody really ever learned how to lead a transformation by reading about it. You need to go out and put what we've been talking about into practice. So put down the book, reaffirm your personal commitment, engage your team, and then distill a version of the ACT process architecture that will work for your team to create both safe passage and an ongoing roadmap and catalyst for transformation. Then engage and learn from your people. It's that BIG commitment you make that will get you from your BIG ideas to BIG results.

About the Authors

Michael T. Kanazawa, is an entrepreneur and advisor to global corporate leaders in the areas of innovation, strategy and transformation. Based in Silicon Valley, his career has been shaped by creating disruptive innovations and driving strategic transformations with the world's leading technology companies and global market leading companies. He has also been a founder and owner of two firms that were both successfully built and sold, including the most recent to Ernst & Young (EY), where he serves as a strategy partner and as the global methodology architect of Purpose-Led Transformation.

The central concepts in his work are rooted in putting customers at the center and collaborating across disciplines and diverse mindsets to drive innovation, strategy and transformation. Early in his career, Michael worked in the same maze of cubicles as Dilbert's creator Scott Adams. That experience inspired him to learn from the best leaders who operated more deeply and beyond the "typical" mold of a corporate leader. This has turned into a lifelong quest to build and shape organizations that delight customers in new ways, disrupt industries, and liberate the full capacity of human ingenuity and creativity.

Clients have included Silicon Valley growth companies, private equity investors, and global corporations, such as AT&T, Chevron, Cisco, Intel, PG&E, Schlumberger, Symantec, and Verizon. Michael is frequently referenced in national media and often serves as a keynote speaker at corporations, associations, and universities on the topics of innovation and transformation.

Michael holds a BA in mathematics and economics from U.C. Santa Barbara and an MBA from the Marshall School of Business at the University of Southern California. You can follow or reach him at www.linkedin.com/in/michaelkanazawa.

Robert H. Miles, PhD, President, Corporate Transformation Resources, is a global thought and practice leader in the fields of corporate transformation and executive leadership. He has served CEOs as the principal process architect in over 30 CEO-led corporate transformations. A summary of the major insights from this experience, titled "Accelerating Corporate Transformations—Don't Lose Your Nerve!" appeared as a feature article in the January–February 2010 issue of the *Harvard Business Review* and was recently reprinted in the quarterly "Reinvention" issue of *HBR OnPoint.*

Over the past two decades Bob has pioneered an *Accelerated Corporate Transformation (ACT)* methodology at such leading companies as Apple, Black & Veatch, Florida Rock, General Electric, IBM Global Services, Infineon Technologies, National Semiconductor, Office Depot, PGA Tour, Rockwell, Southern Company, and Symantec, as well as a number of emerging high-tech companies. Bob also is the author or coauthor of a series of books on corporate transformation and organizational effectiveness, including *Macro Organizational Behavior, The Organization Life Cycle, Coffin Nails and Corporate Strategies, Managing the Corporate Social Environment, Corporate Comeback, Leading Corporate Transformation: Blueprint for Business Renewal, BIG Ideas to BIG Results: Remake and Recharge Your Company, Fast;* and now its sequel *BIG Ideas to BIG Results: Leading Corporate Transformation in a Disruptive World.*

Frequently serving as a Process Architect to executive leaders as they plan, launch, and refocus their corporate transformation efforts, Bob helps new CEOs "take charge" and sitting CEOs launch the next major phase in their organization. A trademark of his approach has been the *Rapid, High-engagement, All-employee Cascade,* which launches the Execution Phase by quickly focusing everyone in the enterprise on a shared set of business performance and cultural corporate transformation initiatives for breakthrough results.

On the Yale School of Management and Harvard Business School faculties for many years, Bob taught in the MBA, doctoral, and senior executive programs. At Harvard he was also Faculty Chairman of an innovative two-week residential program that helped CEOs and their teams plan corporate transformations.

He is a cofounder of the Macro Organizational Behavior Society, a convocation of elected global scholars held each year at Harvard Business School. And after a decade of corporate transformation work in Silicon Valley, he briefly returned to academe as the Isaac Stiles Hopkins Distinguished University Professor and Dean of the Faculty to help guide the transformation of the Emory, now Goizueta Business School at Emory University.

Bob served for over a decade as a faculty member at both the Stanford Executive Institute and at GE's Crotonville Operations (where he redesigned and taught all of the executive-level change management modules). He also served on the Editorial Review Boards of *Management Science* and *Administrative Science Quarterly* and on the Advisory Board of the Organizational Effectiveness Division of The Conference Board. He was Chairman of the Organization and Management Theory Division of the Academy of Management.

Earlier in his career, Bob was an Operations Analyst at Ford Motor Company, a First Lieutenant (Armor) in the U.S. Army, Special Assistant to the Director of Research, Development and Engineering at U.S. Army Missile Command, and a Project Manager at the Advanced Research Projects Agency (ARPA) in the Office of the Secretary of Defense. Later in his career he served on the Advisory Board of the U.S. Department of Energy.

Bob received a BS from the McIntire School of Commerce at the University of Virginia (where he served for two decades on the Advisory Board) and a PhD in Business Administration from the Kenan-Flagler School at the University of North Carolina.

He lives with his wife, Jane, in Charlottesville, Virginia, and Chatham, Massachusetts. He may be reached at RMiles@CorpTransform.com. His website is www.CorpTransform.com.

Index